UNSTUCK

REFRAME YOUR THINKING TO FREE YOURSELF FROM THE PATTERNS AND PEOPLE* THAT HOLD YOU BACK

LIA GARVIN

*Spoiler Alert: Some of these people are you.

For my husband, Wes, and daughter, Maya,
my partners in crime in this adventure we call life.

TABLE OF CONTENTS

FOREWORD

BY RACHEL SIMMONS

WHEN I WAS OLD ENOUGH to sit in the front seat of my mom's Chevy, she flew into full Jewish mother-protection mode. Each time she stopped the car short (which was every few traffic lights; she had a lead foot and was easily triggered), she would throw her arm across my chest as if to be a second seatbelt.

The book in your hands is like having my mom in the front seat, except this time the Chevy is my job and the arm flying across to protect me is Lia Garvin's hard-earned, actionable wisdom.

I first met Lia while working at Google, where I designed a women's leadership program. Lia raised her hand to support the initiative, and within minutes, her insights made our work more impactful. It didn't hurt that she slayed me along the way with her humor. I have hitched my wagon to Lia's star ever since.

In my two decades of researching girls and women, I'm most struck by the paradox many of us live: On the one hand, we have more opportunity than ever before. On the other, we are sandbagged by outdated expectations of what, and who, a woman should be. One of my favorite insights on this comes from my friend Courtney Martin in her book, *Perfect Girls, Starving Daughters*: "We are the daughters of feminists who said 'You can be anything' and we heard 'You have to be everything.'" It's a killer, right?

In the workplace, being "everything" often means walking an impossible tightrope—knowing exactly when to show "agentic," or masculine, qualities like assertiveness and self-promotion and when to revert to the "communal," or feminine, qualities society told us were the "proper" way "good girls" act. "Everything" means having an overactive radar that tells us when to lean in and be assertive and when doing that will rub Dave from marketing the wrong way.

The energy we spend figuring out just how much space it's okay to take up and whether we might get nailed for doing it is a brutal tax men simply don't have to pay.

And the tightrope doesn't just take our energy. It can mess with our minds, too. When you spend all your energy trying not to plummet to the ground, you don't notice that everyone else on it is female. You forget you're not the one who strung up that tightrope in the first place. When you start to teeter, you yell at yourself instead. Stand straighter! Tighten your core!

Unstuck will help you reframe the challenges that arise on that tightrope, especially our tendency to blame ourselves and be imprisoned by impossible expectations. It will remind you to get pissed off at the society that built that tightrope in the first place.

Lia's advice is radically practical. It is efficient and instantly actionable. Best of all, once you learn to reframe, you realize you have a new muscle you can flex anywhere, anytime. It is a resource that regenerates; you get to keep it forever.

Dear Readers, how lucky you are to step into Lia's Chevy and let her take the wheel for a bit. Note: She is a much better driver than my mom. Enjoy the ride!

INTRODUCTION

I USED TO THINK I had a superpower I lovingly referred to as "my Spidey sense." It's that thing where you have your radar on at all times, searching for all the things that could possibly go wrong so you can get ahead of them way before they become a problem. This was a legitimate superpower for me throughout most of my career. Show me a team that couldn't figure out how to get their work done before a looming deadline, and I'd show you a list of risks, dependencies, mitigation plans and communication milestones all with conditional formatting, formulas and pivot tables before you could finish saying "We need a spreadsheet." This superpower helped me thrive in roles working with teams large and small within some of the most influential companies in the world including Microsoft, Apple and Google to launch cutting-edge products and inspire groups to work effectively together through change.

As a coach, this superpower helped me tune into my intuition and immediately recognize when there was something bubbling beneath the surface, allowing me to get to the root of a problem while connecting with people on a deeper level. It made me more empathetic and curious about the goals, dreams and struggles of others and helped me do all I could to support them in getting to where they needed to be.

Not a bad superpower if I do say so myself. OK, not as cool as flying or invisibility or remembering people's names as they introduce themselves instead of completely zoning out, but beggars can't be choosers.

But my superpower had a shadow side. And this is where things started to get interesting (and by interesting I mean terrible). With my Spidey sense on high alert, I was constantly "proactively anticipating" problems in my own life. Anxiety? Check. Lack of confidence? Check. Loud inner narrative telling me I wasn't good enough? Check check check. I would constantly worry about what might go wrong if I took a risk or tried something new, then beat myself up if I tried the thing and it went poorly. When I didn't try the thing, I'd go into FOMO mode and kick myself for missing out on something that might have been awesome. I would hesitate to raise my hand for opportunities, fearing making mistakes or failing while simultaneously shaming myself for being so risk averse. It was an unproductive and futile pattern, and no amount of conditional formatting could help free me from the trap. In a word? I was stuck.

By talking with more and more women, I learned I wasn't alone in feeling this way. And it's no surprise why. As we will explore throughout the course of this book, the slew of double standards and biases we face in the workplace feed into a narrative of feeling like we're not good enough, don't measure up and need to transform from situation to situation to meet the changing expectations of every colleague, manager and leader. Women who are *too* nice are seen as weak, *too* smart as intimidating, *too* assertive as bossy—when *too* is completely subjective depending on whomever the hell is bothered by it. So yeah, it gets really hard to take in all of these pressures but not be *too much* of anything—to need to have your radar on for opportunities to put yourself out there...but not *too* out there.

When it came to the teams I was working with, this garbage super-power (Spidey sense and I are no longer friends), the one that helped me anticipate problems other people didn't even know existed, was also worn down by being hyper-sensitive to all of the issues on teams that could be made better, that were holding people back from being successful in their work, that were making people feel excluded. I saw managers and leaders try to make the changes I was suggesting, and saw just as many look right past them. I saw women not being afforded the same opportunities as men, continually interrupted and talked over in meetings, constantly made to feel like they weren't cut out for the work and how much worse it was when additional dimensions like race, age, sexual orientation and disability were added to the mix. It wasn't fair, and just "sensing" it wasn't going to fix it.

If I've learned anything from superhero movies, apart from the fact that Robert Downey Jr. is and will always be the best, it's that the real superpower is not the ability itself—it's knowing when to use it. As I looked across all the situations I was stuck in, and as I talked with countless women about similar struggles, I started to see a combination of the societal pressures, patterns and people (including ourselves) holding us back, resulting in a set of limiting perspectives about what we could and couldn't do. The more we bought into these limiting perspectives, the more stuck we felt, and the shitty cycle kept reinforcing itself.

This is where the concept of reframing, the central theme of this book, becomes our new superpower (sorry not sorry, Spidey sense). Reframing is the ability to look at a situation where we feel stuck and consider all the other perspectives available—perspectives that would help us get, well, unstuck. Spoiler: perspectives are unlimited and infinite, so yeah, it's way better than the Spidey sense.

When we reframe, we ask ourselves, "What am I missing?" "How else can I look at this?" "What else is possible?" This allows us to think expansively and own our own frame instead of getting stuck looking through the narrow frame some asshole is holding up for us. And this includes when that asshole is *your own* inner narrative.

In *Unstuck*, I will dive into the 12 biggest challenges I've faced and seen women struggle with most in their careers, examine why we get stuck and explore a set of reframing tools and strategies to overcome them. *Unstuck* gives you a new set of rules to play by, from handling feedback to talking about the impact of your work to negotiating for what you deserve—rules that are created on your terms and allow you to be authentic to yourself. My goal is to present a wide range of alternative perspectives to consider whenever you don't know what path to take, or believe there are no good options, or think you're not good enough, or can't make decisions, or whatever whatever whatever shitty thing you say to yourself when you're feeling stuck and show you there's another way to look at the situation. Bonus, it might even help you remember a name or two because you're focused on the person introducing themselves instead of your own shit.

Each chapter includes stories from my experiences with the 12 challenges (names have been fictionalized), examples from authors and leaders that have shed light on new ways to look at them, strategies I've developed to work through them and an exercise at the end to practice what I'm preaching before you move to the next concept. If a particular story or tool doesn't resonate with you, I encourage you to consider why you might feel stuck in the challenge we're exploring in that chapter, put your reframing skills to the test and consider a new perspective that might serve you in that situation. This book gives you a real and personal account of how reframing can be used as a tool to get what you want out of life. But the only way for me to do that authentically is to write like I talk, which means I'm gonna drop some F-bombs when things get heated and if I'm writing in all caps that means I'M YELLING AT YOU.

I started this book writing about one specific topic (Feedback. It's the worst, right?), and the more I explored it, the more I recognized how many of these challenges and pitfalls are connected, leading me to create 14 chapters that all build on each other. You'll see many concepts that appear more than once, because are you really gonna tell me that fearing negotiating has nothing to do with confidence? The chapters are connected because ALL OF THIS SHIT IS CONNECTED, on the pages, at the workplace and certainly in our minds. The issues women face are complex and a lot of the challenges we must overcome are interwoven or built upon or compounded by one another, creating a sticky, murky mess that's incredibly difficult to navigate. So if you're sick of hearing about topics like feedback by the end of the second chapter, forgive me, because the meat (or tofu) is gonna touch the veggies.

I also want to state at the outset that I realize I'm making generalizations about men and women that might not ring true for everyone and that are reflective of my experience as a white cisgender woman. The patterns and challenges we'll talk about may take different shapes depending on your background or how you identify, or what stage of your life and career you are in. Ultimately, I'm here to share my story along with a tool that I have found to be invaluable, and I hope it provides you with a fraction of the clarity, confidence and courage that it has for me.

So join me on this journey to explore the power of reframing, a tool to get unstuck in even the stickiest of situations. There is always another perspective—it might not be easy, it might not be comfortable, but when we think beyond what we've *already* thought of, we find that the possibilities are limitless.

WHY DOESN'T SHE JUST FOLLOW THE RULES? "WHY?" BECAUSE I TRIED IT THAT WAY, AND IT DIDN'T WORK.

CHAPTER 1

HOW IT BEGAN

BZZZT. I flipped over my phone and felt my stomach drop. "Noooooooo!" I screamed, as my husband looked over with dread. I read the text out loud. "hi lia and wes! i'll be moving back into the house at the beginning of next month, so you will need to move out."

I remember it well, not only because it happened recently, but because we were curled up on the couch, having finally put the baby down for the night. We were happily done with all of our prep for the week and enthralled with a gripping episode of HBO's *Succession*. Little did we know at the time this would be an episode that would take us weeks to finish, ultimately having to wait what felt like an eternity to find out if Kendall finally took down Waystar RoyCo.

Forget the etiquette of our landlord evicting us by way of text message; they could have spared us the emotional roller coaster sprung on us by NOT opening the sentence with an exclamation point *(hi lia and wes! good news, you're homeless)*. Like, could they have given less of a shit? We'll explore my disdain for ill-timed exclamation points later, don't you worry.

We paused the show, took a deep breath and started to take stock of what we had to do in the next 30 days: find a new place to live, pack all of our stuff, move WITH A BABY and find an entirely different place to replant our roots.

I immediately moved into a panic-ridden, problem-solving mode, a state I find myself in all too often. My husband and I weighed all of the options and decided a bigger change was in order. We chose to take this situation over which we had no control as an opportunity to "choose" something and settled on moving about 50 miles north to the town where I grew up so we could be closer to family. As right as the decision felt, it brought to the surface an even more difficult conversation I would soon have to have—the one with the manager that I loved about having to leave the team.

For the next few days, I agonized over how I would approach the conversation, wanting to give her as much notice as I could, while also wanting to articulate my regret about having to spring this on her as eloquently and authentically as possible. I felt stuck in a guilt spiral: guilty for creating a disruption in the team, guilty for making a decision that rocked the boat in a role that was otherwise going smoothly, guilty for disappointing my manager.

And then, minutes before we were scheduled to meet, a lightbulb literally went on in my mind (OK not *literally*, but I use this word this way a lot so you may as well get used to it now), and I realized, *What the hell am I sorry about?!* I was rehearsing my talking points of being *so* sorry, and *such* a disruption and waaa waaa waaa I'm *so* terrible, completely discounting the fact that not only was I kicking ass in my work, but there were plenty of potential solutions I could propose to my manager in order to stay on the team. It was not binary.

At that moment, I drop-kicked the frame of "I'm the worst and there are no options for me" I had been using to look at the situation and picked up a new one. This new frame was grounded in what I brought to the table and the possibilities and potential created by thinking outside of the box. I came into that conversation with a mindset of *This unfortunate thing happened, and since I love this team and am awesome at my job, let's find a way to work together to get through it.* And my boss met me right there.

We moved into problem-solving mode together and spent the next few days mapping out a solution for my role that ended up being BETTER than what my job was before I received that fateful text from my landlord.

In this I learned a very important lesson: Even when a bunch of shit is thrown our way that is out of our control, getting stuck in the limiting perspectives of not wanting to let someone down or already assuming we know how they are going to respond ONLY MAKES IT WORSE. If I hadn't reframed, I would have bowed my head in defeat and walked away from a great job, one that had the flexibility to work somewhere else and a manager who appreciated me.

Getting stuck often means thinking we *already know* what the outcome is going to be in a situation, so why should we even bother? This limited thinking ignores the reality that we can't predict the future, and therefore we're likely to be as wrong as the psychic I visited during college who said not to worry, my medical school education was paying off (nope, wasn't in med school) and I was on path to becoming a doctor (zero plans of becoming a doctor).*

*There's 50 bucks I'll never get back.

When we try to guess what will happen based on what we already think, we get stuck. Instead, we have to think beyond the realm of what we already know to open an infinite set of possibilities that weren't visible before.

REFRAME TO RECLAIM

Reframing is the act of looking at a situation that has you stuck from a different perspective. As author and speaker Wayne Dyer said best, "When you change the way you look at things, the things you look at change." It's recognizing the multiple paths and realities that exist simultaneously so that you can evaluate a situation objectively and determine how to best proceed. It's like when I went to the Puff Daddy & the Family concert in seventh grade. Everyone at school was dying of jealousy that my friend and I got to see them, and it was shaping up to be the best night of my middle school life. But when we got to the concert, our seats were so bad we were literally seated behind the stage.* Not good backstage where you are a part of the action—I'm talking nosebleed seats where you see the back of the scaffolding of the set as opposed to what's on stage.

*I mean literally literally this time. I use it both ways. Stick with me.

If we think about these terrible seats as a metaphor for facing any situation where we're dealt a bad hand, we can draw a connection to reframing. From each seat in an arena we see or hear something different. The people in the front experienced Puff and Mase, the people on the sides experienced the dancers, and the people in my seats got to see none other than Busta Rhymes changing costumes. Everyone is at the same concert, but their vantage point shapes their experience.

If you find yourself stuck in the nosebleed section of a problem, especially if it's a situation you don't have direct control over, consider: *What can this vantage point offer me? What can I learn from it? What might I consider for next time?* At the time, I wasn't able to do this with the concert. When we got to the show and saw those seats, I felt horrible. I thought to myself, *Why did I come here on a school night?* and *Who the hell would buy these terrible seats?* I was so focused on what was wrong with the situation it ruined the experience. Imagine how different it would have been if I had the tool of reframing—I could have focused on how awesome it was to get to see a behind-the-scenes view of a concert or how great the music sounded live (even if I couldn't see the stage). But I didn't; I was stuck in a negative perspective.*

Reframing helps us get unstuck from a self-deprecating spiral (guilt, fear, judgment, doubt, avoidance...you name it) where we only see one shitty path forward. When that is your frame, the path usually involves shrinking down or puffing up, or what I like to call "I'm wrong, they're dumb." Brené Brown, the goddess of storytelling, vulnerability, courage and leadership, refers to this spiral in her book *Daring Greatly* as "shame and blame." Brené (in my dreams we're on a first name basis) describes shame as "the intensely painful feeling or experience of believing that we are flawed and therefore unworthy of love and belonging." Blame, as she describes it, is "the discharging of discomfort and pain. It has an inverse relationship with ac-

*My need for reframing goes WAY back...

countability." When we find ourselves in a situation that's uncomfortable, we have the tendency to either shame ourselves (*Why am I not good enough?*) or blame others (*Why did they do this to me?*). It is completely passive and clouds our judgment, making it difficult to find a clear path forward to get through an uncomfortable situation.

It's also the easy way out. As a place many of us tend to go automatically, it is the path of least resistance. It is familiar.

So today, I ask you to stop doing this. Like, right now.

You picked up the book. Fabulous first step, I must say. :)

Now, step two—make a commitment to reckon with the limiting perspectives you've internalized due to all of the shit the world throws at you on a regular basis and choose a new frame entirely. One that doesn't apologize for asking a question or sharing an idea or wanting something awesome for yourself, or whatever you perceive "rocking the boat" to look like. What perspective rocks the boat in the direction that best serves YOU? Whatever you *just* thought of that seemed kind of exciting and terrifying at the same time, that's the one.

TRY ON A NEW FRAME

I'm going to talk a lot in this book about strategies to bring the mindset of reframing to all aspects of your work. Doing this requires retraining your thought patterns, the way you react, how you respond to yourself and how you show up to the challenges you face. It starts by paying attention to what happens in your mind and body when you feel stuck.

To bring this to life, in a moment I'm going to ask you to put down this book and close your eyes. Visualize a large heavy frame that is draped around your shoulders, weighing you down. It is old and cracked. There's paint chipping off of it. It's nothing you'd ever hang up in your house or apartment by choice.*

Grab ahold of that frame by the sides, stretch it up into the sky, and chuck it away from you as far as you can throw it.

Then choose the frame that brings you joy, confidence, power and certainty that you want to wear in its place. As you imagine this one, what's different? What color is it? How is it decorated, and are we doing rainbow glitter or classic gold sparkle? What weight does it have resting on your shoulders? What are you now able to say yes to? What is possible that wasn't before? This is the frame to come back to any time you start to feel that old splintery one starting to materialize. In becoming aware of the thoughts, feelings and reactions holding us back, we can take action to reframe our perspective.

*I'm all for garage sales, but this frame came straight out of the garbage.

Quick reminder of our steps:

- Notice the frame that is holding you back or leading you down a negative path.
  (Ex: Thoughts like *why me, what will others think, I'm not good enough,* etc. and feelings of tightness, tension and shortness of breath)
- Visualize ridding yourself of the frame (aka throwing it across the room).
- Imagine the new frame that appears in its place.
  (Ex: "We can do hard things," courtesy of the brilliant Glennon Doyle)
- Identify the perspective of possibility the new frame

offers that will better serve you.

(Ex: *I'm a fucking BOSS and getting through this shitty situation gives me the confidence to know I can get through the next one,* and the feelings of lightness and ease in your body)

OK, time to practice. Set down the book and give it a whirl. GO!

How did that feel?

As women, we aren't always given the luxury of choosing our frame. Historically, our realities have been presented to us as binary choices—family or career, thin or fat, bossy or submissive. Of course, these aren't choices so much as labels. These labels are reinforced so many times throughout our lives that we start to believe there's no way out. We get stuck.

So we have to materialize our own frame and keep doing it, even when it's hard. That is what I hope to help you achieve with this book. My career has been full of twists, turns, moves, disappointments and let-downs. Countless times, whenever I set boundaries, pointed out a situation that seemed unfair or asked for something, people looked at me like *Jeez, what the hell is her problem?*[*]

They were implying, *Why doesn't she just follow the rules?* "Why?" Because I tried it that way, and it didn't work. Playing by the rules made me more and more stuck, making things continually not work out the way I want them to, further reinforcing my "not good enough" narrative.

So now, we're going to toss aside the perspectives others

[*]*Even when I asked really nicely.*

have imposed on us and explore a new set. Brace yourself and get ready to reframe 12 challenges that I've seen myself and countless women get stuck in over the course of my career because I want to see you get every single thing you want from *your* career and more. It's time to make it happen.

"CAN I GIVE YOU SOME FEEDBACK?"

Literally pack my shit
into a box and
escort me outside
because I cannot handle
this right now.

CHAPTER 2

REFRAMING FEEDBACK

LET ME START by saying I've read A LOT of self-improvement/ leadership development books, especially ones directed at women. You might even say too many. While I feel like I can grab a lil' nugget of something I want to try out from any book in the genre, there is one title in particular that went from being something I initially scoffed at to a playbook for professional success in areas I wanted to develop. Bonus: It really put the power of reframing to the test.

How Women Rise by Sally Helgesen and Marshall Goldsmith is a professional development book for women anchored to a maxim coined by Marshall: "What got you here won't get you there." In short, the behaviors that helped lead to your current success won't continue to serve you in achieving your future goals. It's essentially your standard leadership development book, including several hundred pages of things that seem totally simple and straightforward but then when you try them yourself, people look at you like *WTF is her deal?*

When I first read the book, I was in the midst of a frustrating period at work. I was trying to break through to the next level of my career and kept being told "no." I felt like I had already been actively avoiding the pitfalls listed in *How Women Rise*, but instead of being celebrated for it, I was told I was pushing too hard or that I needed to slow down. Not only did I feel embarrassed and ashamed—I also thought the book was a bunch of bullshit; it was just telling women to act more like men, instead of recognizing the importance of some of the empathetic and connection-oriented aspects of femininity that men should embrace.*

*This is up until the point at which we actually do act more like men, and people are completely put off by it and tell us to settle the fuck down.

So yeah, not a fan.

Then about a year later, a few colleagues at work said they read the book and it changed their lives. These women had been falling into the same pitfalls and were grateful this book had put that internal conflict into words and shared actionable tips for overcoming them. *WTF?* I thought. *I read that book, and I did those things, too, and I got nowhere. I did not rise.* I felt stuck. I picked the book back up, this time throwing away my skepticism, and tried to meet it with all the excitement my colleagues had. I came away with a few pitfalls to work on (fuck it, all 12, every one of them) and a few pats on my own back for things I'd already come a long way in overcoming (fine mayyyybe like one of the 12 if I'm really reaching).

What was at the root of this flip-floppery? As I reflected further, I realized my discomfort with *How Women Rise* was centered on my aversion to feedback, and it was going to take reframing my relationship with feedback to be able to really listen to what it was telling me to do differently.

THIS SHIT IS **HARD**

Of all the places we could have started, why begin this book by talking about feedback? If we're going to examine some of the patterns that hold us back from achieving what we want in our careers, we sure as hell have to get better at recognizing them. As you read through the examples, stories and tips, there might be some moments of "Shit, I do that too. Now I have this to worry about?" Your immediate response might be to close the book, uncork the rosé and get back to watching *Selling Sunset*. But that doesn't sound like we're embracing feedback, now does it? Instead, let's reframe that into, "Wow, I do that too! I get to get better at some of these things I've been stuck on," knowing you have someone to walk right alongside you to figure it out together.

If it's in this book, I have been there, I have done it and I have lived to see another day. Recognizing the thoughts that hold you back *is* an act of internalizing feedback—it's step one on your journey to getting better at it.

Our response to feedback is at the center of our thought patterns. Our thought patterns inform how we make decisions, and our decisions frame how we look at life and its challenges. If we come at feedback from a place of resistance and aversion, it's no wonder we find ourselves stuck when it comes to all of the other obstacles we have to overcome. We all have a story of feedback gone wrong, and while befriending the thing that has stabbed you in the back might take some adjusting, it's kind of a critical first step if we want to achieve anything awesome in our work. Sorry, I don't make the rules. But as I've explored feedback in more depth, I've learned that my love/hate (OK, mostly hate) relationship with feedback stemmed from a misunderstanding about what it is (a tool) and how I can wield it (with genuine interest for its value).

Feedback is hard. Sometimes it can make us wonder how many other people noticed that one *thing* about us, how many times we did that *thing*, what impact that *thing* might have had on the opportunities we've missed or been passed up for.* The wondering can be deeply painful, and sometimes in wanting that pain to go away, it's easier to turn away and reject the concept—as in, *I mean, what do any of those people know anyway? They don't know, books don't know. I don't need any of this shit.* Not the most productive line of thinking.

We often view feedback strictly as a message that is delivered to us, but it can also be a message we are telling ourselves about ourselves. "I'm too sensitive, I take things too personally, I keep getting stuck on the same things over and over. If there were only a way to get unstuck...." As I was reading *How Women Rise*, I realized I had been doing things that were holding me back, and I didn't want to hear it. I didn't want to face it. I didn't want it to be true. So as a mode of self-defense, I blamed the book, which was *clearly* at fault.

I was feeling stuck, and instead of looking inward at the frame I was wearing, I looked outward at all of the

*It's always the one thing we totally already know we are doing and have been actively trying to stop doing. It can be as small or trivial as snorting when we laugh, the use of "irregardless" when "regardless" worked just fine because it's an actual word (or is it?!), the octave to which our voice rises or drops when we're nervous. Who even is that talking? Stop looking at me!

things that made me feel bad about the feedback I had heard. It took looking over at my colleagues, who were all gleaning something really positive from this book, to shake me back into reality and push me to examine the frame that was holding me back. When I reframed the way I was looking at feedback, I was finally able to appreciate it. Or at least start the process.

LET'S PLANT SOME TREES

When we receive a piece of feedback, good or bad, we are essentially given a window into how we are being perceived by someone else. The thing about perception, though, is that it's not right or wrong: it simply is. If someone perceives you as kind, that is what you are to them; if they perceive you as defensive, well, then you're that to them too. *No I'm not,* you're *defensive!* See how that works? The problem is, without feedback, we have no way to know where we stand with someone else, and we have no insight into how we could change our behavior or actions to become the best versions of ourselves.

One of my all-time favorite books on feedback is *Thanks for the Feedback* by Douglas Stone and Sheila Heen. (Who has more than one favorite book on feedback? Me, that's who.) Digging into the fundamentals of why feedback is such a fraught topic, Douglas and Sheila begin by explaining that feedback is everywhere, whether we realize it or not. Feedback can be as trivial as someone smiling at you in the line at the grocery store or giving you the middle finger after you cut them off on the freeway (never happened to me...). And, of course, it can be the tougher stuff like telling a partner you think it's time you started seeing other people or informing a direct report they need to improve their performance in an "or else" kind of way.*

*Or the hardest of all, telling someone you don't want to see the pictures of their camping trip that they're super excited to show you because you just realized you don't care.

One of the central themes of *Thanks for the Feedback*, and what I urge you to anchor yourself to as you think about your default response to feedback, is that it is simply a data point. Again, feedback is not inherently right or wrong, and it does not necessarily signal that we need to immediately change something about ourselves; it is a data point signaling how we are being perceived. Feedback that comes from one person is a single data point; the more times you hear the same kind of feedback, the more you might consider that what's being called out as a perception is actually a reality. I mean, it's just math at that point. Bear in mind that this is true for both positive and constructive feedback, so when you get a bunch of data points telling you your work is awesome, it's time to start listening.

Let's start with a positive example, since so many times with feedback, we focus on the negative. Say you are terrified of public speaking. Whenever you do it, your nerves take over and no matter how hard you practice, you never feel like you landed the delivery quite right, or you didn't speak with enough confidence, or you blacked out on the intro and opened your talk with "We are gathered here today" as if you were officiating a wedding. But after giving an update in a large team meeting, someone comes up to you and says, "That was a great update, super clear and to the point." *They're just saying that to be nice*, you think, shrugging off the positive before resuming your shame spiral. Then a few weeks later, the organizer of the meeting asks you to speak again. They say they received a lot of positive feedback on your last talk and that the leader of the team wants you to give a recurring update. (Winning!) Now you have at least three data points suggesting to you that you're actually kind of good at this speaking-in-front-of-groups thing.

You now have two options. You can a) choose to believe all of those wonderful people who thought you are good at public speaking are full of shit or b) grab that shabby-ass frame dangling around your shoulders telling you you're not good at public speaking and throw it out the fucking window. Please choose b). It's time to start internalizing the positive feedback and stop letting your self-doubt consume you.*

Constructive feedback, on the other hand, can be harder to swallow for some of us, but that doesn't make it any less important. In fact, it's kind of more important. If we're being perceived in a way that is not how we intend, we need to know so we can course correct. Is experiencing constructive feedback still totally uncomfortable and hard to hear? Hell yes. But is that moment of discomfort worth the potential growth? You bet your ass it is. We can't grow if we don't know. Put that on a T-shirt.

If you're anything like me, when you receive constructive feedback, you get a sinking feeling of shame in the pit of your stomach. You wonder how many other people thought this and how much damage this thing has already caused. Then the shame grows, the rumination switch flips on and it's a regular self-judgment bonanza. This happens to me quite a bit, whether it's something I'm already aware

*It's also important to note you can be good at something you don't enjoy doing. A lot of us are "good at" driving in traffic or washing dishes. Hell, I'm great at biting my nails—I'm doing it right now—but it doesn't mean I'm going to make a career out of it.

of and am working on, something I had never thought of and am totally blindsided by or something I am confident is not accurate and wouldn't have been concerned about at all but now can't stop thinking about.... *What if the not-accurate thing is something other people think, too?!**

*It's like when someone says to you, "You know what I love about you? How you just don't care." I'm sorry, what? Like, don't care about which part? My job? My credibility? My appearance? Because each of those are things I spend all kinds of time caring about.

Hearing feedback can also be hard because besides reckoning with something you have to work on about yourself, you now have ONE MORE THING to add to your already filled to-do list. We're maxed out, we're overscheduled, we're already trying the best we can—it can feel like too much. *Really? Now I have to add "delegating better" to my list? Can I delegate that feedback to someone else, please?*

But as they say about planting trees, the best time to plant a tree was 20 years ago; the second-best time is today. Something like that, right? All you can control is today. Sure, it might have been helpful to have heard that piece of feedback the minute it was first observed, but the next most helpful time to hear it is RIGHT NOW. So what if other people noticed the *thing* you're doing? Knowing about it means that you can work on it, or stop doing it, or start doing it—whatever *it* is—and choose to try and improve for the next time. But you can't make a choice to change if you don't even know what you might need to adjust. You can't grow if you don't know. So good I said it again.

SERIOUSLY, IT'S NOT ALL BAD

Feedback has a relatively negative connotation for most people because we tend to only think of it as a bad thing.

I don't think there is any more dreaded question in the workplace than, "Can I give you some feedback?" *Literally pack my shit into a box and escort me outside because I cannot handle this right now.* But is that the response we want to have when we're striving to get unstuck from these situations and be the best version of ourselves? Rhetorical question—the answer, dear reader, is <u>no</u>.

When we start by framing feedback as a personal attack, we close ourselves off from being able to hear what is being shared (and, by default, learning what course of action might be required if we want to change). When this is our frame, we generally go in one of two directions: We either completely ignore the feedback or we overinflate the importance of it. Neither course of action brings about quality growth or change.

Internalizing positive signals about what we are doing well is just as critical to our success as knowing what we need to improve. If it's not broken, we don't need to fix it, and my guess is there is so much less that is broken than you're giving yourself credit for. While we each bring our unique tendencies (*cough* baggage) for how we brush off positive feedback, I have found three of them to be the most prevalent.

First, our tendency to look for criticism in the positive. When your boss says, "Great job on this month's report," you wonder, *Oh no, what about last month's report? It must have been terrible since she didn't bring up that one.* Let the compliment sit. She liked the report, and if she had an issue with last month's, she would have said something.

Our second tendency: We miss the positive behavior that needs some reinforcing. Let's say your boss expands on the report example and does bring up last month's report: "Great job on this month's report. You included a lot more specific examples than in previous months, and it helped give the stakeholders who receive the report much more context on the project." When we hear this, ignoring the positive, we jump to, *I knew it, my manager thinks I'm the worst.* Reframe! She thinks you've significantly improved upon your work without her needing to ask you, and that's kind of awesome and deserves recognition.

Finally, when we only listen for the negative, we're always waiting for the other shoe to drop. We are stuck in a continual cycle of holding out for the (often non-existent) bad part of the message, never taking a moment to celebrate what is going well. We hear "Nice job on this month's report..." and then our brain adds a silent and contradictory *buuuuuuut...wait for it, here it comes*—a reflex triggered by our self-defeating subconscious that won't just stop talking and let us enjoy a compliment ONE TIME. This makes us so much more susceptible to burnout and resentment, because we never feel like we're doing a good enough job even when people tell us we are.

Many of us—especially hard-working, perfectionist-leaning, professional women—tend to downplay positive feedback and get stuck overanalyzing the shit out of the negative. What if we were to instead take up a frame where both have equal weight? One that shows we're composed of many qualities, some of which we are excited about, others we're working on, and all of which are OK? This is one of the areas I work on most, professionally and person-ally, including my embarrassment over receiving the feedback that I "take feedback too personally!" How meta is that?! *Why can't I just let things go? Why does this bother me so much? Why haven't I gotten over this? Why do I even care? Why, why, why, why, why?*

These self-deprecating questions, all unsolicited DMs from my inner critic, have not helped me move ONE iota closer to accepting the fact that it's an area I'm working on. In fact, each time I berate myself with these questions, I actually feel worse.

We have to stop doing this to ourselves. Immediately.

THE ALL-KNOWING INNER CRITIC

Your inner critic goes wild when it hears constructive feedback, whether it's about something we knew about and were actively trying to overcome (*see, I told you so*), or something we are completely blindsided by (*oh yeah, you're bad at this too*). It might take many shapes, but whatever it looks like, you know it when it's there. The inner critic is the voice that lingers over every confident decision and says, "Yeah we could do *that*, but like, what if it doesn't work out and we're totally embarrassed and no one likes us anymore? Not judging, just asking." The one that says to keep things professional but, "You know, you could smile more," or, "*Was* the unicorn emoji appropriate in that email to the VP?" There is no winning when this voice is present—we're too much and yet not enough all at the same time. Thanks but no thanks.

In this book, we will keep exploring the inner critic because, like it or not, it's present every time things get interesting in our lives. The inner critic is sneaky. It gets smarter as we get wiser and has been with us through thick and thin. Its motive is to keep us safe, and it loves the status quo. Each time we get a step closer to accomplishing a goal or taking a risk, its voice grows louder, more persistent. But if we want to reach our full potential, professionally and personally, it's important to first thank our inner critic for its service and then break up with it. *It's not you, it's me. OK, it's you. Now get the hell out of my life.*

First things first, we have to recognize when the voice is present by discerning between rationality/thoughtfulness (good) and criticism/judginess (not good). The inner critic generally talks in terms of absolutes—"I always...," "I never..."—and lays on the victim mentality pretty thick. It can also be mean. *Really* mean. It can talk to us in ways we'd never talk to someone else, insulting our intelligence, our abilities, our body and our potential. When we recognize a negative thought pattern, we have to stop it in its tracks. It's not feedback, it's just a loop—an endless cycling spiral of self-defeatism.

Start paying attention to how you talk to yourself, what thoughts creep up as you approach a risk or consider taking on a challenge. Be mindful of when the voice starts to show up (saying things like, "This is too risky, this is never going to work, who do you think you are," etc.). When you hear it, take a deep breath and divert your attention away from the negative. Consider what opportunities this risk or challenge might afford you. What might it teach you? What is exciting about it? In what ways will it tap into your strengths?

Because our inner critic takes on an ominous presence, disguising its voice and its needs and desires as our own, it can be really helpful to depersonalize it and remind ourselves that the critic *isn't actually us.* As you start to become more mindful of your negative thought pattern, also pay attention to what the voice sounds like. This can do wonders to loosen the grip our inner critic has on us. Does its voice resemble that of a teacher, parent or other important figure in our childhoods who told us we weren't good enough? Does it resemble our own voice at a younger stage of our lives, beating us up over a mistake made or path not taken? Does it have a name, a shape, a smell?* Personifying the inner critic reminds us that it's something outside of ourselves, which gives us more authority to tell it to get lost.

*Mine smells like my seventh grade locker room and constantly reminds me I don't run the mile fast enough.

In the book *Playing Big*, a field manual for women on how to realize their full potential, author and leadership coach Tara Mohr offers another perspective—that the inner critic has all of the best intentions in mind. Its goal is to keep us safe. It just comes on a little too strong. The catch is that the inner critic is seeking safety at the expense of being accurate, fair, in touch with reality or understanding of the greater forces at play, making it *kind of* the worst possible force to protect you. Solid, solid effort, but the execution lacks follow-through.

Tara offers another more optimistic strategy for dealing with our inner critic—to tap into what she calls our "inner mentor" to stand up taller against it. Our inner mentor is the badass, powerful force that lies within all of us. It's the confidence and self-assuredness that takes on whatever challenge our inner critic might inevitably question, and it's the force that will help us get through it. Using the same strategies we used to personify our inner critic, we can paint a picture of our inner mentor and ask ourselves how they would handle a difficult situation we are faced with.

My inner critic is always telling me I don't think through things enough...even though my long history of *overthinking* things would argue otherwise. Ironic, right? When I'm stuck in a rut and am focusing too much on these limiting beliefs, I turn to my inner mentor, who looks exactly like present day Jennifer Aniston (who somehow keeps getting more beautiful and badass as time goes by), and she gives me the strength to just. fucking. go for it. My inner mentor is the version of me who has already been through this shit and seen the other side; she knows that when I trust my gut and bet on myself, I can't lose.*

*Disclaimer: If your inner mentor does not kick the imagined situation's ass, you haven't materialized a badass enough mentor. Keep trying. Think Beyoncé tearing shit up with a baseball bat.

Sometimes we don't realize our inner critic has been talking to us until we've already handed over the reins in shaping our decisions. In these instances, creating a simple ritual to check in with ourselves and access the inner mentor, like glancing at the Wonder Woman figurine I have on my desk at work, can snap us out of a spiral. Once we stop the inner critic from stopping us, it's easier to reframe our focus on what matters, like being ready for the next challenge life throws our way. And right now, that challenge is FEEDBACK.

LET'S BE HONEST (AND EMPATHETIC)

I mean, if we were all great at giving feedback, it wouldn't be so painful to receive it, now would it? Yeah, we're terrible at giving feedback, and it's time we pay it forward by building some skills. One of the most popular books on the market about professional feedback is *Radical Candor* by early Google employee and management consultant Kim Scott. Her feedback framework is simple, easy to remember and works for both positive and constructive feedback. Kim's book describes a matrix where "saying nothing" and "challenging directly" are on one axis and "caring personally" and "not caring at all" are on the other. The sweet spot for feedback falls in the zone of caring personally and challenging directly. Kim suggests we enter a feedback conversation from a place of empathy, while providing actionable insights that a person can take with them. This framework is especially helpful for those more difficult conversations, because when we approach them with empathy, understanding where the other person is coming from or what they might be experiencing, the person on the receiving end sees that we're sharing feedback for the right reasons.

With this approach, any hard message becomes infinitely easier to deliver because the receiver sees that you are looking out for their best interest and are not making assumptions or jumping to conclusions. Bringing empathy tempers the reaction of "You don't even understand" because you just demonstrated you *do* understand (or at least seek to). If you're having trouble figuring out how to land a hard message with empathy, consider how you might want to hear difficult feedback if you were really struggling (Disclaimer: The answer cannot be "not at all"). What would need to be said in order for the message to best land? While you and your inner critic could lead a MasterClass on how to make someone feel shitty about feedback, think about how you might give feedback if you brought a little compassion to the message.

In his book *No Rules Rules*, co-authored with professor and cross-cultural communication expert Erin Meyer, Netflix co-founder Reed Hastings discusses some of his strategies to make giving and receiving feedback both safe and effective. Netflix uses a tool called Stop, Start, Continue, which suggests people share one thing a person should stop doing, one they should start doing and one they should keep doing in order to be the best version of themselves at work. To do this effectively, it has to be a given that you will follow the rules of *Radical Candor*, providing specific examples and sharing feedback with someone because you care, not just because something they did irritated you.

I have found this Stop, Start, Continue framework to be really helpful, especially when working through team-wide challenges. Discussing behaviors a team needs to change using this framework depersonalizes examples and pushes people to be more specific and actionable in their suggestions. It's also great for delivering feedback to a manager or person senior to you, as it keeps the feedback concise and action-oriented.

How does it work in practice? So glad you asked. I had a manager once who tended to respond to things only when there was a problem. He was a busy guy and operated under a "need to know" way of sharing feedback, meaning everyone on his team was to assume everything was fine until otherwise noted. But if you're a person who needs a little "good job" dopamine hit to keep you going, you could go long stretches of time really fiending for that positive signal. While being managed by him, I had yet to learn the Stop, Start, Continue framework, so from time to time I'd go to his office after we had a successful meeting or a project had been completed, and drop awkward hints like, "So that project...wow, done already, two weeks ahead of schedule...was there anything...?" Eventually he'd get the hint and say something like, "Yep, great job!" and I'd return to my desk, knowing he would have raised an issue if he had one but glad to have that validation for my own personal sense of closure, even if I nudged it out of him. Yes, I was a grown-ass adult engaging in this song and dance, and yes, I know, I missed the opportunity for *actually* addressing the issue. This is what avoiding feedback leads to!

A reframe sure would have saved a lot of time right there. Had I been in on the Stop, Start, Continue framework at the time, I might have suggested that he *stop* the habit of only responding to emails when course correcting is needed, *start* sharing nuggets of positive feedback when he feels it's warranted to help motivate the team and *continue* making himself available to troubleshoot issues and brainstorm solutions when we do run into problems. Not so scary after all, right? What I like about this framework is the "continue" step gives you an opportunity to call out positive behavior you want someone to keep doing—and acknowledges there is *always* a way to find a kernel of value in something someone is doing (even in moments where it's really, excruciatingly hard to isolate).

As you've learned by now, it is important to share feedback on something we observe, to speak up, to challenge AND (not but) to show you care about that person so they can internalize it. It's also important to make feedback clear and actionable so someone can change the thing or keep doing the thing. I like to pair these frameworks with one last model: the Situation-Behavior-Impact (SBI) method developed by the Center for Creative Leadership. The SBI method encourages feedback givers to share the situation in which the issue occurred, the behavior that needs course correcting or reinforcing (remember, all feedback frameworks can be used with positive feedback!) and the impact of this behavior. For example, "In the meeting this morning (situation), you interrupted to 'mansplain' a point I had literally just finished making (behavior) and it made me want to punch you in the face (impact)." Or something like that.... Let's look at another example, this time a positive one. What might you say to thank the person who stopped the mansplainer? "In the meeting this morning (situation), you called out when someone interrupted me as I was making a point and asked me to continue (behavior), and it gave me confidence to keep speaking by validating that what I was saying was important (impact)." This method helps you get specific because if you're mentioning something for all three parts, you can't help but be clear.

Even armed with these tools, a wide range of biases can come into play when sharing feedback, because it's hard to differentiate our perceptions of people's behaviors that are based on our personal preferences from those that are impacting the work. If your inner critic is running wild before giving feedback, that's actually not a bad thing. When it comes to putting our biases in check, the second guessing of "Should I even say this?" is a healthy and critically important question to be asking. But that question should come with a healthy dose of "Will saying this be helpful to this person?" The beauty of building more comfort in feedback is it makes confronting your own biases easier.

As you build confidence about giving feedback, know that even the best feedback framework might not apply in all situations, and the power dynamic in the conversation might mean you have to get a little more creative when delivering a hard message. But having these tools at our disposal ensures we enter feedback conversations prepared. With all frameworks, the most important thing to anchor to is empathy. The more you demonstrate an understanding for where the other person is coming from, whether they are sharing feedback with you or you with them, the better the conversation will go. It allows people to combat defensiveness, ask thoughtful questions and internalize a message.

FIGHTING THE DOUBLE STANDARD

What about messages riddled with bias? Women are constantly faced with a double standard at work and are continuously walking a tightrope of what to change about ourselves to be who others want us to be. When you introduce more dimensions like age or race to that same tightrope, it's like asking women to traverse it on a tandem bike with someone who's peddling in the opposite direction. The system is broken and I don't have a simple solution, but we sure as hell aren't going to fix it if we don't continually push against it.

Let's say a manager shares feedback with a woman that she spoke up too much in the past few meetings—the question becomes, what was the impact? Did some kind of issue occur as a result of her taking more airtime than others in the meeting, or are we witnessing a personality judgment based on an archaic belief about how women should communicate? To answer this question, it's always helpful to ask: Would this same feedback be given to a man in this scenario? Spoiler alert: No. Research shows both men and women overestimate their perception of how much airtime women take up in meetings, meaning we're often double-judged when we chime in to make a point. We can't catch a break.

Biased feedback typically goes a lot deeper and taps into intersectional (multiple dimensions of identity) factors like race and gender. Stereotypes around being too quiet and timid, or too assertive and direct often reinforce the double threat of gender and racial stereotypes, as well as confirmation bias, otherwise known as interpreting new data as confirmation of our existing beliefs. Confirmation bias can also hit the feedback giver. Because of the myriad of double standards we will discuss throughout this book, when hard feedback is given by a woman, it often impacts how we think about the woman more than how we think about the feedback. With the biased belief is that women are too sensitive or too critical, feedback shared by a woman could be seen as harsh or judgmental. *She's so critical and nitpicky. She's kind of a bitch.* The same feedback shared by a man? *He's tough, but he knows what he wants. He's a good guy.*

The truth is biases are present in any situation we're faced with: They are a product of how we're socialized. Pushing against the system means we ask for more information so that we're holding others accountable for keeping their biases in check. We stay mindful of the way we are communicating and recognize the role we play in reinforcing these patterns, call out false stereotypes and biases when we see or hear them and enlist our allies in majority groups to keep an eye out and support us in speaking up.

Feedback is the lifeblood of understanding how we can be our best. Awkwardness around feelings, social norms, comfort with being direct and all sorts of communication blunders can dull the effectiveness of it. That doesn't make it any less important. Develop your personal tools, positive reinforcements and frames for how you find comfort in both sharing and receiving feedback. Do what you need to do to fight your inner critic, and prepare yourself to fight bias with an objective eye and an open mind. And then pick up your shiny new frame, wear it proudly and get to work on being your best self.

PUTTING IT TO THE TEST

I have found that when I'm working through a sticky situation, I spend much of the limited time I have beating myself up over and over (rumination for the win!) as opposed to strategizing how I can move forward.

Cue the exercises.

Spend the last five minutes of each chapter on yourself, and by the end of the book, you will have a wide breadth of tools for applying reframing to all aspects of your life and work.

LET'S PRACTICE

Think about a time in the recent past when you had feedback you wanted to give to someone but didn't share it. Maybe it was to a parent, a friend or a colleague. Take a few minutes to write down what you wish you had said if you didn't have a filter on.

First, what was that filter about anyway? Is it saying you don't deserve to ask for what you need? That you're too clingy? That if you say it no one will like you?

To quiet these thoughts, turn to your inner mentor and incorporate the tools we talked about in this chapter (empathy, context, specificity, action orientation, removing bias) and rewrite the statement you just wrote.

How does it read now?

Is it more in line with something you might be willing to share? If so, what's stopping you from sharing it? If not, how can you keep dialing up the empathy, context, etc. so that it gets there?

When we look at it objectively and remove the emotion, anger and judgment and weave in the empathy and specificity, feedback doesn't have the same sting as we feared it would have.

Writing it down helps us stress test it, prepare for how to frame and deliver the message and take an opportunity to think ahead about any follow-up questions the receiver might have. It also quiets our inner critic because we often see what we wrote down is so much more palatable than what we were imagining in our minds.

Whether you share it or not, you can see that you do have the capacity to articulate feedback—you just had to reframe.

NOT ALL HEROES WEAR CAPES, BUT WHEN TALKING ABOUT YOUR WORK, WEAR A FUCKING CAPE.

CHAPTER 3

REFRAMING YOUR IMPACT

THE EVIL SECOND cousin of giving and receiving feedback is the act of talking about your work and its impact. If the thought sends you into a wave of panic, you're not alone. As women, we're often told throughout our early years not to talk about ourselves, not to brag, not to show off. Then we become adults and we're supposed to sing our own praises? *I just finished rolling my eyes at Stacy for talking about herself constantly—now you're telling me* I *have to do it. Seriously?*

Yes, my friends, you do. Talking about our work is something we have to collectively get better at. We are the owners of our own destinies, and no one is going to have any clue about the greatness we can achieve until we tell them—this means without diminishing, underselling or—and this is key—laughing about it.

Ah, laughing.

Before I wrote this book, I wrote another book about account-ability in teams. It was like the chapter you will read later on about reframing accountability, only 10 times longer and way more dense (you're welcome). When I started writing it, I was captivated by my idea, and the words flowed freely from my fingertips. But when it came to *talking about it out loud*, I couldn't do it, it was *not happening.*

Just saying the words "I am writing a book" out loud took me MONTHS, and I still kind of squirm when I have to squeeze them out. I was initially encouraged to write the book by a former mentor, who was instrumental in helping me gain clarity in my messaging. When I asked, "Why can't I tell people I'm writing a book? What is it? What am I afraid of?" I got the response I expected. He chuckled, then deadpanned, "Because people will look at you like you're a cliché." Everyone and their mom says they're writing a book and few people have anything of value to say. What made me think I was different?

Noted. OK, so that was one data point.

Then I went to my manager, one of those once-in-a-lifetime managers who unconditionally supports you, who had been encouraging me to lean into my writing. I told her about my plan—except all I managed to say was "I am writing a boooooo—" before bursting into laughter. But she got it. And then she did that thing all great mentors do: she gave me some feedback.

"That's awesome," she said. "Now say it again without laughing." *About that...* yeah, that proved to be much more difficult. Like, literally 30 uninterrupted minutes difficult, until I finally said "I'm writing a book" one time through with a straight face.

Now that I had my sea legs, I tried to say it to another colleague in a meeting where my manager was present so she could see me in action. I managed to get the words out without laughing (win!), then asked why that colleague thought I might be having such a hard time saying it. Was it because people would think I was a cliché? "That's not how I see it," she said. "I think it's the fear of claiming you are the authority on something. That can be vulnerable, as in, what if people don't agree with you?" Then she said something that made me smile: "I would love to read your book, by the way." My first fan. Progress.

Looking at these three inputs, I had some interesting insights to consider. I appreciated my mentor's initial blunt response. His implication that everyone in the world was writing a book helped ensure I would approach mine in a thoughtful, original way. My manager helped me come to grips with the fact that yes, I was writing a book and no, that wasn't a laughable idea. And my colleague hit the nail on the head regarding what had me laughing about writing in the first place: it *was* a fear of talking about my work, of owning my expertise. My laughter was a way of deflecting whatever backlash, pushback or even disinterest in expertise that might follow.*

Summoning all the Jennifer Aniston and Beyoncé confidence I could muster (yeah, two inner mentors were required here), I pushed forward and wrote the 40,000-word first draft in a remarkably short timeframe. I celebrated. I cheered. I told my inner critic to "fuck off." Then, a few weeks later, I read it again. *Yikes, this is what all the fuss was about? Maybe I should have reined in my celebrations a bit until the second re-read....* I enjoyed the process but wasn't loving the words on the pages (kind of

*I mean, what if people don't like it, think I'm weird, no longer want to be friends, and soon, because I told people I was writing this book—on a subject I'm not even an expert on since I'm not an expert in anything at all ever—every single person in the world wants nothing to do with me?!

important), and came to terms with the fact that the book I'd started was going to end there. And that wasn't my inner critic talking—it was me. The time I spent away from the book gave me insight into what I actually wanted to do. Which was to write a book! Just not *that one*. And that's OK. Because I wrote this one instead, and on most days I can talk about it out loud without laughing.

YOU ARE THE EXPERT OF YOU

Talking about our work brings up all sorts of baggage. As women, we are socialized from a young age to carry the weight of conflicting ideals: to both be perfect but not a show off; to be hard-working but to make it look effortless; to be smart but not *too* smart. Be everything to everyone but don't you dare take credit for it or talk about how awesome you are. Fuck that! These unachievable contradictions suffocate us! Then we grow up and people wonder why it's hard for us to talk about our work and sing about our accomplishments. Um, how about, maybe because we were told *not to*, FOR DECADES?

Hoping that people will be magically aware of the work we do and why our contributions are important is a pattern many of us get stuck in. It's difficult to find the balance of ownership vs. collaboration vs. humbleness vs. boastfulness, and what we often come up with ("I'm pretty OK, I guess, as long as you think so, mostly.") articulates only a fraction of the impact we actually have. Because of this, it can be tempting to avoid touting our work completely, and/or to wait patiently and politely for other people to notice. We think to ourselves, *I'm working hard and others are benefiting. Why make it a big deal? Great work speaks for itself. Right? Right?!*

Bueller?

The short and correct answer is a big, whopping NOPE. IT DOESN'T.

Everyone has way too much on their own plates to remember all the things we did. People's own work and their own feedback are consuming their thoughts. That *thing* you created for them four months ago might have *actually* slipped their mind.*

People need a friendly reminder. When we avoid talking about the work we did (*and* why it matters), we let our inner critic take hold and repeat the mantra that it wasn't important anyway. The frame telling us that a) talking about ourselves is bad or braggy and b) good work always gets noticed, will directly contribute to stagnation in our careers if we allow it to go unchecked. No one is better equipped to talk about why what you did matters than you are. Own your accomplishments. Ground your work in the impact it created for your organization. Let go of the frame around your shoulders that says you shouldn't speak up for yourself or command too much attention.

Sometimes people will notice the work you're doing, and that's fantastic. Some managers or leaders keep an eye out for their people, maintain notes of behaviors they want to reward, praise individuals when they do something great or give stellar performance review feedback that sets them up for success. But most do not. And here's the thing: relying solely on other people to notice your hard work is a cop-out. If you can't speak with clarity about what you've done and why it is important, most managers will question

*You're welcome, by the way.

if it was *actually* important at all. Not speaking up for yourself can be interpreted as a lack of effort or interest in the work, which leads to the assumption that you're not really invested in the outcome. Reminding people about the awesome work you're doing in a thoughtful way is not only OK, it's expected.

When I used to work in design firms, the advice given to every new designer was the same: defend your work, be able to explain what you did and why you did it. Presenting a design concept and saying, "Yeah, I just kind of thought this looked cool," leaves the client underwhelmed and leads them to question your credibility and expertise. But if you were to say, "When designing this, I started by focusing on the company's mission, and what they stand for; I used the idea of 'teamwork' to inform the PMS swatches and shape languages I explored, and came up with three options that embody the spirit of the company...." Um, yeah, I'm going with the second one, even if I don't know what the fuck PMS swatches are.

BRING IN SOME BAIT

You might assume you only need to talk about your impact during performance review time. You assume wrong. We need to be talking about what we are doing and why it is important ALL of the time. When recognition of your work comes at a frequency of exactly ONE TIME a year, you run the risk of people turning around and saying, "Wait, what? She still works here? On *this* team?"

The first place to start talking about your impact is in a feedback conversation. While these can feel like one-way conversations, they *are* conversations about your work, so you've got to come with ammunition. Remember the designer's framework. Do you want to say, "I did cool stuff, mostly, I think," or, "These are the four ways in which my actions have directly led to a 16 percent increase in sales and improved employee retention?" Use a conversation with your manager to share some of the awesome things you are doing, incorporating them into the process by asking for feedback so they feel invested. In other words, bring in some bait.

Let's look at a scenario with two dialogues. The first is what I hear people come in with ALL OF THE TIME, and the second is an alternative to try, with a lil' reframing sprinkled on top.

SCENARIO: *You are halfway through the year and want to get a sense of where you stand.*

YOU: "Hey, manager. I've been working extra hard this year, like *around the clock*, and wanted to know where you think I can improve."

MANAGER: "Hello, employee." *Looks caught off-guard, then gazes longingly out the window for a moment.*"Yes, let's discuss all that. Sure. Yes. So I haven't had the best visibility into your work, but who couldn't benefit from improving their public speaking skills? We all have room to improve there, right? Good talk!"

YOU: (not getting any of the actual feedback you wanted because this note was essentially summoned haphazardly from a list of general things anyone could work on at any time): "OK great, will do. Byeee."

The meeting ends. Nothing is accomplished. Neither of you will ever get those 30 seconds back.

Where did things go wrong?

For starters, you were completely vague about the things that are going well. Adding how you've been working "extra hard" seeds an undertone of defensiveness or even entitlement, like, *"Hey, I'm working hard; you better go soft on me."*

Let's try this again, shall we?

SAME SCENARIO:

YOU: "Hey, manager. We're about halfway through the year, and I wanted to check in. Strong presentation skills are critical for my role, and they are something I have been spending a lot of time working to develop. Last review period, I was nervous when presenting and have since made a conscious effort to seek out more opportunities to present in front of groups and have been doing practice sessions with one of our team members to help me feel more confident. What feedback do you have about my presentation skills or any other aspects of my work?"

MANAGER: "What a pleasant surprise, I love sharing feedback on a specific example!" *Ignores the window. Leans forward with excitement.* "Yes, presentation skills are important for your role, and I'm thrilled to hear you are both in tune with that fact and have been making progress there. I'll keep an eye out for opportunities to attend your presentations so I can support you and offer any feedback."

By taking the initiative to point out your strengths and weaknesses, you took control of the narrative, showed your manager precisely what you were working to improve and set yourself up to receive relevant feedback (and maybe a bit of coaching) in the future. Amazing! People who are invested in helping you succeed appreciate having a hook to grab on to. It gives them an opportunity to support you in an area you proactively want to develop. It also demonstrates you don't just wait around until someone stops you in your tracks and asks you to go in another direction; you're self-aware and can reflect on your own about areas in which you can improve. Best of all, by using the feedback jiu jitsu technique of asking an open-ended question, you allowed them to step up and do their job as a manager of sharing actual useful insights.

Coming to your manager and just saying "I'd like to improve" is meaningless. It's better than claiming you have *nothing* to work on, but without meat on the bones, it feels hollow. Well, yeah, we all want to improve. We'd also like to get paid more money and end world hunger while we're at it. *What else?**

The same goes for telling your manager how hard you are working without sharing any examples. "Hard work" is subjective and means something different to everyone. What one person finds difficult, another person might find completely effortless, depending on their skill set, experience, interests, etc., so put some of that hard work toward keeping a running list of the stuff you work hard *on.*

*We also might be debating how much money we can save in order to casually dip out of this daily grind of a job without having to move back into our parents' basement. That part doesn't go in the story to your manager.

A tip I've shared with a colleague who was struggling with talking about her work: write a summary at the end of each week of all the things you accomplished and share it with your manager, indicating that no response is required. If anything seemed like a quick task in theory but actually turned out to be more involved in practice, add another sentence explaining what went into it—the additional planning, a bit of course-correcting, organizing follow-up meetings, you name it. It's a simple task, and it gives you the opportunity to frame your own story. This helps a lot in situations where you might have spent a lot of time on something that hasn't yet resulted in a tangible outcome, like if you spent a large part of your week trying to build stakeholder alignment around a decision and then the executives' meeting was cancelled. You could write the weekly summary and add a line to the effect of "no decision was made," or you could describe some of the elbow grease involved on your part. Regardless of the situation, the words "literally achieved nothing" should never be the default.

Another tip: DO NOT, I repeat, DO NOT ever list a bunch of shit on a status report that took you less than three minutes to do. "Changed the title of a slide," "printed a document," "made a folder"—these tasks do not belong in any kind of summary where you're trying to communicate how hard you worked. You might as well add "wasted the limited time we have on this precious earth by forcing you to engage with this useless minutiae."*

*Mom appreciates when I print documents for her, even if you assholes don't.

WATCH YOUR LANGUAGE

So what do you write in that status report now that "made a folder" is officially off-limits?

Consider for a moment the last big project you finished that you are really proud of—something you had a major role in making happen, not something that happened on your team that you were tangentially aware of. Imagine describing that project to someone, paying close attention to how you talk about your role specifically:

First question: Did you describe yourself as "helping out"? A huge pitfall women fall into is using "helping" to describe their work, as if your career is synonymous with making cookies for a neighborhood bake sale or painting your neighbor's fence as a quick favor. HELPING OUT IS NOT A JOB. Your job requires skills you have cultivated over time, something you are likely an expert on and, most importantly, something you get paid to do. It is not a volunteer project.

Instead of using the word "helped," use powerful language like "led," "drove," "authored," or "strategized." Put this book down and immediately update your LinkedIn profile to get rid of "help" and all its variants. Want to show you are a strong collaborator? The word "collaborated" does the trick just fine.

When we diminish our work, talking about it as if we were loosely involved, we confuse the people evaluating our current or future potential work and we weaken the authority of our impact. It doesn't make you sound like a strong partner or a great team player—remember, we have the word "collaborated" for that—all it does is make you sound like you sat on the sidelines and didn't do anything important. Not all heroes wear capes, but when talking about your work, wear a fucking cape.

Second question: Did you describe yourself as "we," as if you teamed up with two or three of your clones to get the work done? Take a seat. When talking about your own individual work, there should only be one subject, a.k.a YOU. Don't believe this is a problem? Look at the last 10 emails you've sent or that have been sent by a woman at work. How many of them use "we" to describe something that pertains to a single person (the sender)? All of them? I'm guessing it's close.

"We" are expert collaborators and bridge builders, sure, but throwing "we" into the mix bars you from taking credit for your amazing ideas, and a lack of confidence in the work is often the takeaway. You might be thinking, *This sucks, it isn't fair to talk about what I did when I worked with a group of people on something.* Does it suck, though? The inner critic we talked about at length, the second guessing, the double standards we face with celebrating our achievements—those forces are what tell us to hold back when talking about our work, not the lack of importance of our contribution. Stop listening to that shit. This is your time to shine. Embrace it.

Third question: Did you use the word "just." As in, "I just wanted to ask a quick question," "If I could just grab a moment of your time," "I was just thinking...."

What's so bad about "just?" In 2014, tech executive Ellen Petry Leanse published a blog post about her observations of the word "just," sparking so many views and shares it even landed a shoutout on *The Today Show*. After being fed up with hearing the word over and over in meetings, she decided to run a little experiment on the differences in the use of "just" among men and women. Whelp, the results weren't great, ladies. Ellen says, "I am all about respectful communication. Yet I began to notice that 'just' wasn't about being polite: It was a subtle message of subordination, of deference. Sometimes it was self-effacing. Sometimes even duplicitous. As I started really listening, I realized that striking it from a phrase almost always clarified and strengthened the message." Strike that shit RIGHT NOW.

I'm not going to say I've removed the word from all of my communication, and if you're reading the e-book version of this, I'm guessing you've already done a search for the word "just" to laugh about how much of a hypocrite I am. It's a work in progress. But instead of being blissfully unaware while I proceed to diminish myself, I now have a process to check in. Before you send out an email or answer a question in a meeting, think twice before using "just."

In *Playing Big*, the book that introduced us to our inner mentor, author Tara Mohr explores why women use speech patterns that downplay our messages. She discusses the paradox women face, reminding us that "women need to do more than our male counterparts to come across as both warm and competent. We likely need to be more deliberate about continuously conveying warmth even as we are demonstrating our competence." The problem is that the "helping out," the "we" and the "just" language chips away at our demonstration of competence. In the immortal words of DJ Khaled, "Congratulations, you played yourself."

And since I'm a big fan of "helping out," help me help you help yourself. Whether it's putting a giant Post-it on your laptop with these words crossed out, getting in the habit of double checking your emails before sending them or asking a trusted colleague to be your diminishing language sponsor, find a way to break the habit of using these words when talking about your work and its impact.

Last question: Did you throw self-restraint to the wind when using punctuation? This portion of the conversation wouldn't be complete without talking about good ol' smiley faces and exclamation points. The tools of the gods, the symbols we rely heavily on to joust with that passive aggressive d-bag who just asked us why we haven't finished the thing he literally asked us to do five minutes ago. *I'll get right on it! Thanks. :)*

I went many years avoiding smiley faces and exclamation points in all forms of communication, first with texting and then with emails. But alas, working in the corporate world, they reared their ugly heads in my effort to communicate warmth. While you won't catch me using either when talking about my work (like you will never catch me using Reply-All in emails with more than six people*), I use them non-sparingly (read: all the time) in work emails.

In the spirit of watching our language, rein these in as well. A smiley face once in a while isn't going to tank anyone's career, but 14 exclamation points in a three-sentence email plus a "byeeee" could start to call into question whether or not you should be kept on the payroll. ;)

*The 30-person team doesn't fucking care you will be 15 minutes late to work today because your chiropractor had a last minute cancellation.

WHERE THE RUBBER HITS THE ROAD

Speaking of payroll, effectively talking about your work and why it matters is not just a nice skill to have—it impacts your bottom line. Since performance reviews are the ultimate forms of feedback and talking about our work, reframing our relationship with them and figuring out how to ace them is critical. Most jobs have some kind of performance review mechanism, and I'm guessing that once it gets going, talking about your work has a tendency to shift from mild annoyance to full *Panic Room. Lock me away, it is not safe for me out there.*

In many companies, there is a hidden set of rules around performance reviews that you only learn about if someone who has been there long enough to have "beat the system" shares them with you—things like how much content to write, who to ask you to give peer references if those are included and how many smiley faces or exclamation points are acceptable before your manager prints your review out and tears it in half.*

Of all the things that make my blood boil about workplace culture (and as you will learn over the course of the book, the list is *lengthy*), performance reviews are up there. There is a precise number of review systems that I've seen adequately assess a person's job performance and potential and it aligns with the exact number of scrubs the members of TLC wanted to engage with: none.

The answer is none, my friends. None.

At their best, performance reviews help people reflect on their past work and have a conversation with their manager about opportunities to make more of an impact over the next review cycle. Fine, whatever, that's a worthwhile exercise to run through once or twice a year. But at their worst, they can breed toxic behaviors. For instance, systems that stack rank can create anxiety and competition. Systems that rely heavily on peer reviews can create popularity contests where people begin campaigning for support. Worst of all, systems that collect anonymous 360° feedback can leave people feeling blindsided by all the things people don't like about them that no one ever told them.* In the end, you are left with an organization of people primarily working to game the performance review as opposed to doing the right thing for the company or their team at any given time.

*It's the "burn book" from Mean Girls except the stakes are real and Regina George controls your ability to get a raise. Not fetch. Not fetch at all.

I am a firm believer in changing both the system and how we respond to it, so in response to my disdain for the performance review, I spend countless hours coaching women on how to talk about their work, ensuring they too can play by the unwritten rules that need to be followed in order to win. I boiled down some of the gems people have found into the following nine steps, which I have conveniently coined as the "Narrative in Nine."

Talking about our work requires thinking in terms of the story behind it. Ask yourself:

1) *What was the state of the situation before I got involved?*

2) *What contextual information would someone need to understand who knows nothing about me or my work, my team, etc.?*

3) *What problem was I solving?*

4) What was my role in the project?
5) What was my unique contribution?
6) What if I or my team had done nothing?
7) What were the consequences of the course of action I took?
8) What decisions or impact did my work lead to?
9) What consequences did my work help to avoid?

Clear, concise answers to all of these questions help construct a compelling narrative around why what YOU did matters. And since we know our work better than anyone else, why shouldn't we want to be the one to tell the story?

Regardless of whatever promotion process a company has in place, we generally tend to think we're ready for that promotion *looooong* before our manager agrees. Between biases, quotas and a general sense of too much going on to notice our work, there are many reasons we might get passed up for that promotion even when we think we've nailed our work. Nine times out of ten I've seen that the default response, no matter who your manager is or where you work, is "you're not ready." It's often said with very little thought, an involuntary reflex managers have that leaves us bowing our heads in defeat and hoping to try again next year.

But let's be real for a moment: managers can also get jaded by the eager beavers who ask for a promotion every 15 minutes. Ran an effective meeting? Time for promotion! Sent a detailed email? *ahem* Where's my promotion?! So if this is you, simmer down and answer those Narrative in Nine questions I shared to land a powerful message about your work before diving into the formal review process.

Whether it is for a review, job interview or networking event, we continually have moments where we need to be ready to talk about our work in a meaningful way. There's no escaping it, and that's a good thing. When we're overextended and have taken on more projects that we can handle sustainably (which, let's be honest, is most of us), it can feel like all our work is random. Reject this. Let go of the nihilistic conclusions. Remember the narrative that runs throughout your work. Push past the doubt, ignore the inner critic and know there is *always* a thread that can tie your work together, as long as you find the right (you guessed it) frame.

PUTTING IT TO THE TEST

Reading about telling your story is one thing... writing your story is another.

Deep down inside, we know what we did well. But we can get so lost in all of the layers of doubt and judgment, and finding the right written words to describe it, that the awesomeness of our contribution can often lose all meaning when we put it on paper.

LET'S PRACTICE

In this exercise, we're going to revisit the Narrative in Nine questions I posed about how to tell the story about your work, removing the filter so we can get to the good stuff.

Think about a work project from the past six months. Then explain your contribution out loud or into a voice memo app on your phone as if you were explaining it to a close friend or family member who is super excited to learn all about the things that you do.

REMEMBER TO SPEND EXTRA TIME ON THE MEATY PARTS OF YOUR ACCOMPLISHMENTS, INCLUDING:

- What problem was being solved?
- What was my unique contribution?
- What decisions or impact did my work lead to?

Now think about how you might have described it to a manager or in a performance review. Is it different? What's holding you back from making the second time around sound like the first?

When you center the story of your work on processes, systems, structures and metrics, you don't come off as braggy, inauthentic or too me-centered. You sound like the confident badass you are.

OUR INNER CRITIC HATES WHEN WE SET GOALS, IT'S LITERALLY LIKE, "WHO IS THIS BITCH TO TELL ME WHAT TO DO?"

CHAPTER 4

REFRAMING YOUR GOALS

WE'VE ALL HEARD the advice: Set actionable goals. Set stretch goals. Set meaningful goals. I love the spirit, but HOW DO WE DO IT? In our quest to be the best at all things work and life, we can get caught up in chasing things we don't want or consider important, lose ourselves in the expectations others impose on us or get stuck in the overwhelming space of not knowing where to start. But this does not mean we should throw the pursuit of goal setting out the window.

It's not easy. At all. Our inner critic HATES when we set goals, it's literally like, "Who is this bitch to tell me what to do? Oh, you think you're better than me?" When we let our inner critic take the driver's seat in terms of our goal setting, we play it way safer than we need to. Putting ourselves out there feels like too much effort, not worth the hassle. Sadly, our inner critic says this about things that are actually very important to us, like achieving a promotion or landing a new job, providing yet another reason it's imperative we get a handle on the power it has over us.

Then there are times when we base our goals on expectations *other* people have for us, including people who might have our best interests in mind...and people who, well, not so much. How many of us out there have been working tirelessly toward a goal, only to realize YEARS INTO IT it was someone else's vision or dream? It happens all the time, and it makes us afraid to set goals because it's hard to know what's really behind them. We think we're supposed to have this job (doctor or lawyer), achieve this thing (title or salary) and make this milestone happen (people applauding as we walk through the halls), never questioning if that goal will make us happy or fulfilled.

Other times, it's the change factor that gets in the way. Goal-setting with regard to making a major change can feel so uncomfortable that, even in the worst circumstances, we avoid it completely. In the TEDx talk "Draw Your Future," a talk about the power of visualizing your goals to the extent of drawing a roadmap for them, speaker Patti Dobrowolski says that even when people are faced with a life-threatening choice, the odds are 9 to 1 that people will still be unwilling to make a change in their lives. With such a deep-seated aversion to change even in life or death situations, it's no surprise that when the stakes are a little bit lower, most folks don't even bother with going after what they want.

Whatever your reason is for having a difficult relationship with setting goals, it's time we figure out what will make us happy and successful in our lives and work.

BUT I DON'T EVEN KNOW WHAT I WANT

If you're reading this and thinking, *But I don't even know what I want!* you're not alone. For many of us, just figuring out what to set our sights on, even before we try to attain anything, is the hardest part.

Usually, it's easy to frame it in the negative: we know exactly what we *don't* want. The things that turn us off or make us feel unfulfilled are generally abundantly clear—we can vent about *those* things all day if given the opportunity.* These are the things that demotivate us in our work, lead us to second guess ourselves and make even the simplest task feel like we're running a marathon without access to water or Band-Aids. You know, everything we call our moms to complain about, even though we're adults (allegedly).

The things we *do* want can be trickier to identify. They can feel temporal or situational and imagining what you want in one instance might not be true in another. Discovering what you want requires understanding your values and the beliefs that make up who you are. For example, recognizing that you appreciate connection and community might mean you could flourish in a position that requires you to be social or extroverted; conversely, you most likely wouldn't be happy in a job where you keep your head down and don't engage much with other people throughout the day.

If identifying your values still feels about as abstract as understanding the plot of a Christopher Nolan movie, conduct a mini-research study on your mood to learn what feeds rather than drains your energy. Over the next work-week, keep a log of your activities each time you move from one item on your agenda to the next. At each transition, make a note of your energy level and motivation on a scale from one to 10. Maybe you started the day with a boring status meeting, so your energy level was at about a three

*Your basic "I don't want to commute more than 15 minutes," "I don't want to be micromanaged," "I don't want to have to hear any kind of constructive feedback at any point..." Wait a second.... We already went over this two chapters ago. We love feedback now! :)

coming out of it, but when you had a great conversation with a colleague to brainstorm how to solve a complex problem, it brought you up to a solid eight. Running this experiment for five consecutive days will give you enough data to not only see the kinds of activities feeding your motivation but the kinds of people with whom you should strive to surround yourself.

Armed with this data, you can start to make choices—are there certain projects you can take on that align with activities that increase your energy and enthusiasm? Are there people you can partner with who do the same? Is there a course you can take or a skill you can develop? In developing the interests you are most passionate about, you'll likely meet other like-minded people who share those interests with whom you'll find there's an instant connection. And you didn't even need to swipe right.

YOU HAVE A PURPOSE

Even the most seemingly out of reach goal becomes attainable when we connect it to our values and mean-ingful when we connect it to our purpose. One example is the Ikigai model for finding purpose (from the Japanese word for "reason for being"), which helps us explore the intersections of the things we love (a.k.a. our passions), the things we are good at (strengths), the things that serve humanity (looking beyond ourselves) and the services you can be paid for (a profession vs. a hobby) to find our reason for being, or purpose, right at the center.*

*Spoiler Alert: If all roads lead to you "becoming an influencer," run through the exercise another time.

I found this to be an incredibly helpful model for

ensuring the goals I established for the next stage of my career and beyond because it connected to what was really important to me. When we think about the concept of "purpose," it can seem so abstract and unattainable, but when we deconstruct it into its essential elements, the bigger story becomes clear.

Along with understanding our Ikigai, taking deliberate action to map out your path can help reduce some of the apprehension in setting goals that align with the bigger story of you. *Designing Your Life* by Bill Burnett and Dave Evans uses the power of design thinking to lay out a working route that gets you where you want to be. The authors argue that since many of us might not know how to articulate what our passions are right off the bat, by applying the design framework of thinking expansively and then narrowing down, patterns and themes will emerge, linking things together in ways we might not have considered. Their model incorporates curiosity (anything and everything is on the table), bias to action (jumping in and just trying things), reframing (hell yes, reframing limiting beliefs about what you can and cannot do), being aware of the process (letting go of the goals and seeing what happens) and radical collaboration (asking for help and enlisting others).

Using these two frameworks, I not only found the thread that connected all of my professional experiences, I also developed a new relationship with my goals. When we think there is only one way to be successful or one means of accomplishing our goals, we miss out on all of the great things that could be available to us if we reframe. Instead, Bill and Dave say "there are many designs for your life, all filled with hope for the kind of creative and unfolding reality that makes life worth living into. Your life is not a thing, it's an experience; the fun comes from designing and enjoying the experience." How much more exhilarating is that than feeling like you have to get it perfect on the first try?!

Adam Grant explores the concept of purpose in his book *Think Again*, which examines the importance of challenging and rethinking our default thought patterns. He discusses the tunnel vision we can get when pursuing happiness, the extrinsic factors that create joy and how this can distract us from figuring out what matters to us, resulting in us feeling less happy. *But my athleisure apparel* does *matter to me!* He argues "meaning is healthier than happiness, and that people who look for purpose in their work are more successful in pursuing their passions—and less likely to quit their jobs—than those who look for joy. While enjoyment waxes and wanes, meaning tends to last."*

*Oh I know what you might be thinking: What if my purpose is not to have this bullshit job? I've been there. Dig deeper.

If you think finding meaning in your goals isn't all that important, consider the psychological theory behind Maslow's Hierarchy of Needs, which asserts that human behavior is motivated by five fundamental needs: physiological, safety, love/belonging, esteem and self-actualization. Right above having a roof over your head is the need to belong to a group and feel connected to other people, knowing that you matter and are accepted by others. At the top of the pyramid is the need to feel like you have reached your full potential. According to this theory, when we do not reach our full potential of satisfying our life's purpose, we are neglecting one of the fundamental components of living our best lives. With literally only five needs, missing any one of them is a big fucking deal. No wonder we feel shitty when we're working toward a goal we feel no connection to!

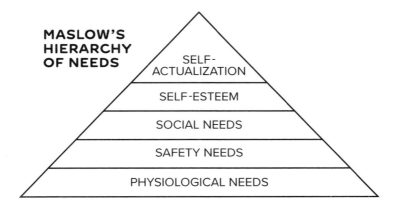

Take a purpose statement like "helping women realize their full potential in the workplace," something I may or may not have considered. When I first articulated it, I thought, *How the hell am I supposed to do that?* But as I began to break it into smaller goals, I started to see a path to getting there emerge. I now had something on paper to react to—what could some potential mediums be for communicating this message? Book? OK, what is the first thing to do? Write? Yep, start typing. Writing the book was hard. Figuring out that I had to start writing in the first place? Much easier.

Humans are purpose-driven creatures, or as Brené Brown calls us, "a meaning-making species." We have to find the meaning in everything we do, otherwise we eventually run out of motivation. Our purpose acts as a north star, and goals set mile markers to keep us on course toward living our purpose. The path is rarely a straight line, but in being clear about our goals, even if we take some twists and turns, we'll stay on the right track.

A LITTLE FROM COLUMN A
AND A LITTLE FROM COLUMN B

Emboldened with a newfound sense of meaning behind our short time on Earth, it's not uncommon to feel a wave of anxiety as you try to figure out how to ensure what you do matters. I'm right there with you. Time is our most finite resource, so there's an instinctual incentive to ensure you're not wasting it when working on your goals. But then you remember all of the conflicting advice you've heard over your lifetime about how to effectively reach these goals and stall out picking a direction to go: *Do I work on my strengths or weaknesses, weaknesses or strengths— please tell me, which is it?!*

The simple answer is: BOTH!

A wealth of research has gone into methodologies on mapping your talents to apply them to the activities you do at work in support of achieving your professional goals. It is clear that when you leverage strengths (e.g., communication, empathy, achievement) in any situation in which they are needed, you see a better outcome. StrengthsFinder (since rebranded to CliftonStrengths) is a popular self-assessment you can use to diagnose your top five "strengths" and then read deeper into how to put these into action at work. As a fan of anything in quiz form—from the days of *Seventeen* magazine's "Is He The One?" to BuzzFeed's "Which *Game of Thrones* Character Are You?"—I gravitated toward this approach right away.* And if I learned one thing about myself, besides that I could always game the quiz to result in Khaleesi, it

*For the curious, my seventh grade crush from math class was inevitably not "the one."

was that when I could finally articulate the superpowers I brought to my work, I felt like the stars aligned in following my passions.

When we play to our strengths, we're on a faster route to getting to what is called the "flow state," the state in which we're in the zone, totally present and the work is effortless. It's how you might feel when you're on a long run or bike ride, playing with your kids or deep in an engaging conversation. Time passes without you even noticing. Flow state is decidedly *not* the feeling of time draining while we're swiping on social media on our phones, only to look up at the clock and see 47 minutes have slipped by. That's a disconnect with the present. But when we're working on something that helps us achieve the goals we have for ourselves *and* it's effortless, we've reached the sweet spot.

While playing to our strengths is a valuable strategy and can get us to this flow state, many times it is difficult to see the connection between what we do well and achieving our professional ambitions. My secret to this is to think in terms of a bird's-eye view of how a strength might relate to the bigger goal or aspiration we have for ourselves before we come to the overwhelming conclusion that we're in the wrong kind of work and it's time to jump ship. One of my strengths involves "risk anticipation." If you're wondering if that's a fancy way of saying "worrying," yes, yes it is. But it can actually work as a pretty valuable skill when it comes to project planning, and it's even more invaluable when connecting it to my greater purpose of helping women realize their full potential in the workplace.

I have had jobs in the past where my personal strength was not welcome because the people around me only wanted to hear everything was fine. For a while, I was convinced this made me bad at my job, because I wouldn't just say "this'll be great!" when my overactive Spidey sense could map out in my mind all of the things that could go wrong. Then, you guessed it, I reframed it! Instead of looking at the granular things that could potentially go wrong on a project, I redirected this strength toward serving the goals of my organization: to make money and deliver work on time; and to my goals: to help getting things done feel more effortless for my team members. I then spoke about risks in terms of those goals, and you better believe my team started celebrating my "risk anticipation" strength.

But now the hard part: Achieving your goals isn't only about playing to your strengths. In fact, Marcus Buckingham, the co-author of the StrengthsFinder assessment, says so himself in the "When Strength Becomes Weakness" episode of organizational psychologist Adam Grant's podcast *WorkLife*. Marcus notes there are times when strengths can in fact be overplayed and become less useful to you in the moment. This is when they can work *against* achieving your goals. We've all seen this before—a person whose strength in seeing the bigger picture has trouble paying attention to the details, the strategic thinker who has trouble with execution.

As a general rule, a combination of recognizing our weaknesses and becoming acutely aware of the things that prevent us from playing to our strengths is the key to success. No big deal, *just* the golden ticket. It can be hard to see the line of a strength tipping the scale into the weakness zone, especially if we are really tuned in with something being a strength. When we deny or hide from these flavors of weaknesses, are embarrassed of them or avoid acknowledging them, we hold ourselves back from reaching our full potential.

For example, if you've determined one of your strengths is

empathy, then one of your weak spots might be feeling over-whelmed by the strong emotions of others. Working on a weak-ness born out of an overdeveloped strength is much more effec-tive than picking and choosing a random, unrelated weakness to work on such as your inability to make a soufflé rise. But, if one of your weaknesses is *discipline*, incorporating time for meticulous precision in baking *could* help you get in the habit of sticking with a commitment. Soufflé it up.

The shadow side to my "risk anticipation" strength I mentioned earlier is *judgment*. When the pendulum has swung too much on one of our strengths and we're stuck in the weakness zone, it can be helpful to think about the ways in which an otherwise detrimental behavior might have served you. For me, *judgment* is my Spidey sense out on a rogue mission—no Spider-Man suit, just jumping around from building to building, stirring shit up. Somewhere in there is a nugget of wanting things to be fair and equitable, but in its current framing, it's gone a little haywire. Recognizing this behavior, I can rein it in and evaluate how I can reframe judgment into curiosity for how to inspire people to recognize the importance of fairness and equity.

With a balanced approach to developing our strengths and weaknesses, we can set meaningful goals that are driven by our intrinsic motivation of purpose. We learn to resist the inner critic telling us to fix a gazillion things about ourselves because we can tease apart what really matters and what is just negative self-talk. And, because it's the gift that keeps giving, it helps us prepare ourselves to receive difficult feedback—we know what to pay closer attention to or what to let go of, all in service of accomplishing our goals.

SEEK THE JOURNEY, NOT THE DESTINATION

It took a long time for me to find the kind of work that leaned into my strengths, felt authentic and that I could find enjoyment in doing. When I finally found it, it was not by accident. It all came into focus when I started setting the right kinds of goals. No one is saying this shit is easy, or that it doesn't take work; but the more intentional we are about understanding ourselves, the more control we have.

While we can't always shape all facets of our careers (systemic and societal biases and inequities play a huge factor in that), we can control the motivators we use to decide what kinds of opportunities to go after. Psychologist Carol Dweck, who I'll discuss further in Chapter 10: Reframing Failure, makes the distinction between the two types of goals that drive our motivation to accept feedback and develop ourselves—performance goals and learning goals. Performance goals are driven by status and achievement; in other words, we want something because it will result in some kind of extrinsic benefit like more money, power or positive reception from others. Learning goals, on the other hand, are driven by the intrinsic motivation of expertise in a skill or serving the bigger aspirations you have for yourself. Think about the difference between getting a title change to show people how important you are versus learning a new skill that can help you enjoy your work more deeply. I'm leading the witness here, and hell if I didn't admit I love a good title bump, but there's a longevity and value to the second approach that will far outlast the addition of "senior" to the title you already hold.

Centering your development on the goal of unlocking new possibilities gives you so much more resilience than tying it to winning or losing. When we go after things so someone else will think we are important, we quickly lose steam when obstacles or setbacks arise because we have no intrinsic driver to anchor them to.*

The inner critic LOVES setbacks, thrives on them. The "I told you so" vibe is at its strongest when something goes wrong. After I graduated college, I immediately signed up for a master's degree program. I knew a master's degree was a good achievement to have, and the idea of having two degrees in the bag by the age of 22 sounded pretty awesome. I was living in Los Angeles at the time, and the program was in Irvine, only 45 miles away (or up to five hours away in LA traffic). I figured it would be fine, I would just commute there three days a week for school and rent a room, and then live my regular life on the weekends. It was fine that I didn't know anyone in Irvine, and it was also fine that I was going to pay for two rents. All fine. I signed up for the program, paid my money and drove 45 miles to attend my classes the first week... only to discover it was *not* fine. The program was in a subject I was not fully invested in, renting two apartments was unsustainable since I had to cut back hours at work in order to go to school, and the isolation was brutal. Two weeks after starting the program, I dropped out, forfeiting all of my tuition for the semester (#finalsale). At that moment did I feel like I was "crushing it?" Not so much. BUT, that grueling drive up and down the 405 sure gave me the opportunity to reevaluate my goals.*

The lesson? Hell hath no fury like the absence of a learning goal. The whole endeavor was attached (and only very loosely) to a performance goal of getting a master's degree in a subject of little interest to me. When I saw

*Wanting the promotion because Katie isn't even that good at her job and you should have been picked is both NOT a goal and has no purpose behind it. Sure, Katie sucks and she robbed you of the spotlight, but without having a clear learning goal to back up wanting the promotion, it's hard to argue why you're more deserving.

*When referring to LA it is a legal requirement to cite which freeway you took to get somewhere.

the hurdles I'd need to jump over to complete the year, it was all too much. Before making a big decision like moving, pursuing an advanced degree or changing jobs, search for the learning goal and make sure it matters to you.

SHAPE YOUR PATH AND START WALKING

In the previous chapter, I mentioned the hesitation I felt about sharing my goal to write a book and my self-doubt in calling myself some kind of expert. Though it was hard to take my own advice, I ask that you never judge your goals for not being worthy, good enough or ambitious enough—or for being *too* ambitious. If you want something for yourself, go after it. It's no one else's business. Isn't that what Taylor Swift's whole *Reputation* album was about? A lot of times it can be a helpful confidence-builder to flesh out some of the steps toward achieving our goals to gain clarity if you still fear skepticism from friends, family or peers, or if you're facing a lot of self-doubt from our old friend, the inner critic.

When we identify a goal and don't make progress toward achieving it, our inner critic often swoops in with a friggin' PowerPoint presentation detailing how we aren't disciplined or motivated enough. In the book *Atomic Habits*, author James Clear debunks this inner critic myth, asserting that when we have trouble sticking to a habit, it's not because we lack motivation—rather, it's a lack of clarity. He argues that when we ritualize or automate decisions that have to be made toward achieving a goal, motivation in the moment isn't even in the equation. When we boil down the steps for achieving a goal or establishing a habit into "atomic" units, the obstacles in front of us become much more manageable. For example: The goal of saving money for a trip requires decisions on what to spend or save day-to-day, how to track spending and potentially exploring alternative avenues for boosting your income with side jobs. Automating these decisions could entail buying a premium ground coffee and creamer so you can make coffee at home without springing for a barista-made coffee (and obligatory $11 avocado toast), or making lunch the night before work so you don't feel inclined to grab it on the go. It could involve downloading a spending tracker app and setting a reminder in your calendar so you look at your finances at the end of each week. All of these rituals are things we do in advance so the small decisions that could set us off track are *already* made for us in the moment.

I've been trying for YEARS to establish a regular habit of meditation because it helps reduce anxiety and has innumerable benefits for my health and well-being. The problem is I only remember to do it when I'm in a meeting at work—not exactly the right time to take five. After several fruitless weeks of trying to get myself to meditate for a measly five minutes a day, I decided to give in, switch up my goal and try for one minute. Now, I wasn't thrilled to start out with only *one measly minute* because it felt so pathetic. *Am I really someone who can't get my shit together and do something positive for myself in the time it takes to debate with my husband about who will unload the dishwasher?** But I wasn't doing it, so I thought, *Screw it, let's start small.*

When I got to work, I'd close my eyes in the parking space and breathe for a minute before walking into my office. At the end of the day, I'd sit in my parked car and close my

*Because those arguments last a LOT longer than five minutes.

eyes again before heading into the frenzy of rush-hour traffic. After dinner, just before opening my laptop to dive back into work emails, I'd close my eyes for a minute. By breaking my goal into smaller chunks, not only did I discover I could find the time—I managed to meditate for 15 minutes over the course of the day, something I would've never thought possible at the outset. I beat myself at my own game.

So many times, when we can't stick with something, we give up on it. One false move, and we're over it. I mean, who doesn't decide the whole day is shot once cupcakes are served in a morning meeting? Literally open the food floodgates. But you don't have to ascribe to that all-or-nothing mentality. We can have half a cupcake and still hit the gym after work. We can adjust, fine-tune, reframe our approach, and as we find our stride, we can work up to more.

Start with a set of small steps to take on the journey toward your goals, ones you can commit to with confidence that feel scary and exhilarating. We know the millisecond we sign up for something whether we will actually do it or not, which is usually the moment we start planning elaborate excuses to get out of it. Don't play that game with yourself. Play a new game, one of accountability and action. Find the thing you will stick with and do that. Then do a little more of it, and a little more...

We will never fully be able to clear away all of the noise, but the more we understand what we want, what matters to us, how to develop ourselves and how to make incremental progress, the more prepared we will be to hit those goals. Aim to feel excited about the aspirations you have for yourself, to resist your inner critic and to think beyond what seems possible today. Shake off the doubts and start doing. You'll like what you find on the other end.

PUTTING IT TO THE TEST

We all have goals for ourselves, whether that's waiting until the weekend to polish off that pint of Ben & Jerry's Americone Dream (shout out to Stephen Colbert and all of his greatness) or as big as becoming CEO of your company one day. Both goals look equally in and out of reach depending on the kind of week you're having at work. Trust me, I get it.

What I'm guessing we don't all have is a prioritized list of our goals that clearly maps out the steps for how to achieve them, and we're going to create that right now.

LET'S PRACTICE

Think about a reasonable goal that you can achieve in the next three to six months but is still a bit of a stretch. No judgment! Write it down.

- Beneath that, write a step necessary to achieving that goal where you feel stuck or haven't been making the progress you want. For example, if getting a promotion is your goal, this step might be taking on projects that are more visible to senior management or having a career conversation with your manager.
- Next, write out five decisions that could be automated in advance to get the ball rolling, e.g. setting up a meeting with your manager, signing up for a stretch project, etc., sorting them by priority.
- Last, assign a deadline to each task and add reminders in your calendar on these dates to ensure you complete each task. Yep! Shit's getting serious.

Notice that all the hard decisions about what to do and which step to take first have been decided for you. It's like magic.

...EVEN WHEN YOU'RE RIGHT, ANNOUNCING YOU'RE RIGHT DOESN'T MAKE YOU <u>MORE RIGHT.</u>

CHAPTER 5

REFRAMING CONFLICT

"What outcome do I want?"

While it's not always (OK fine, *ever*) easy to admit it, we generally know the answer to this question. I find myself asking this most often when I'm in an argument and holding on for dear life to my point that is *so right*, if only the other person would listen. Or when I'm pretty sure I *know* what the outcome would be if I were to say what is burning on the tip of my charged-up, frustrated-as-hell tongue, but I want to say it anyway.*

In the midst of a heated debate, particularly the ones where we believe we are right, it can feel impossible to just take a deep breath and let it go. But doing so can be transformational. The skill of thinking through the extent to which our words or actions impact the people, places and things around us gives us an incredible advantage in our interpersonal relationships. Managing conflict effectively

*And yes... sometimes I say it in spite of knowing the outcome.

is hard! The pressures we are under to be accommodating and never rock the boat can make many of us as wary of conflict as we are of multi-level marketing schemes.*

*If it involves selling energy drinks out of the backseat of my car, consider me uninterested.

Dealing with conflict requires us to self-reflect, something that takes deep practice and attention. It's not easy, especially when we're *super* pissed or feel we've been wronged. So instead, we react in the moment, then beat ourselves up for what we said, hopping on the rumination train to "Why-did-I-say-that-ville." When you're stuck in a conflict and can't see the way out, it's time to examine the patterns you are perpetuating around reactivity or avoidance that are holding you back from achieving the outcome you want.

REACTIVITY IS A BITCH

Pathwise Leadership, a program centered on teaching mindfulness and self-awareness to business leaders, grounds its teaching in the concept of "suspension of attention," the act of holding back 10 percent of our awareness at all times, and refocusing that last bit to our body. When someone says something that upsets or excites you, what happens? Is your breathing calm and measured, your head clear as a feeling of control washes over you? Or do you feel your palms are sweaty, shoulders are hugging your ears and it's been about four minutes since you've taken a breath? The body notices long before we recognize something has impacted us and, like all of us, it just wants its feedback to be heard. Tuning in to its signals gives us a significant advantage in managing a conflict effectively.

Consider the last difficult conversation you were in where you thought of all the perfect things to say after the conversation was over. On your way into your next meeting, were you suddenly flooded with an array of artfully crafted proof points that would have gotten you EXACTLY what you wanted from the conversation had you managed to say them in that moment? We've all been there. All too often, we find ourselves stuck, reflecting *after* reacting, unsure how to move forward.

Suspension of attention is about flipping this so we can build enough self-awareness to reflect *before* reacting. We do this by focusing a fraction of our awareness on the present moment as opposed to letting our full consciousness be hijacked by the situation, whether it's by noticing the feeling of our feet planted on the ground, our heart beating in our chest or the sound of birds outside the window, gleefully chirping away because they don't have to deal with any of this corporate bullshit. Then we take a deep breath and think before we respond.

You know that moment when you're in an argument with your partner, and that *thing* pops in your head that you could say that would really cut to their core, but you know if you say it you will have crossed a line and hit below the belt?*

The closer we are with someone, the more we know what to say that will lead to connection...and what we could say that will sever it. That moment when you think to yourself, *No, I shouldn't go there*, is suspension of attention. While that pause might be just enough time to

*Oh, come on, you totally know that one THING. Such as bringing up anything related to their mom, and how they might sound exactly like she does.

craft the most earth-shattering comeback you've ever thought of in your life, check in with your body—what is going on inside? It's very likely your heart is beating out of your chest, your stomach is in knots and you are so freakin' mad you don't even care about the outcome. That's where the focus on your body comes in; stopping and taking a few deep breaths can snap you back to the present and allow you to think clearly before making a move or saying things you can't unsay.

OH, THE STORIES WE TELL

Alas, when we're in a difficult conflict, it can feel like the whole world is out to get us. But by taking a step back and reframing, we can see there's a *remote* possibility that is not the case. Stanford's infamous course on interpersonal dynamics uses an experiential learning framework to make its students face their fears about conflict in communication head-on. "Experiential learning" means no instructions—in the course, groups of eleven strangers sit in a room for 20 hours with no idea what is going on, and soon people have no choice but to start talking. As people talk, they share their reactions, emotions, feelings and responses in real time. So yes, I finally got to live my dream of being on *The Real World*. It wasn't videotaped, and there was no booze or hot tub hookups, but people did stop acting nice and started getting real, so it was close enough.

One of the main takeaways from the course is the feedback framework of "When you said/did X, I felt Y, and the story I am telling myself is Z." This simple tool puts the ownership of the feeling onto you, as opposed to stating someone "made you feel" a certain way, because the reality is that no one can *make us feel* something. It helps us recognize the difference between facts, feelings and stories: the story is the part that is triggering the reaction, even if the facts present a strong case for the other person being a total douchebag. The beauty of this framework is that it is specific and gives you something to anchor to in order to understand the impact of your words and actions. Brené Brown speaks about this in her book *Rising Strong*, reminding us to consider our emotions, thoughts, beliefs, actions and the sensations in our body when examining the story.

Sharing the *story you are telling yourself,* or the "story that I am making up," as Brené calls it, allows you to take responsibility for the fact that your narrative might not represent the full picture of what is going on, but the feelings about that story are still present and very real (and sometimes very raw). We can use this framework not only to remind ourselves that we are layering a story onto an incident that happened but as a tool to communicate how we're feeling to someone else. In terms of the latter, using this framework indicates to the other person that while your internalization of their action may or may not be what they intended, it is the reality of what you are experiencing.

Let's look at an example to bring this to life. Imagine you just became the manager of a team of your former peers. One of your new subordinates is also a work friend and the transition into managing them is proving to be more difficult than you anticipated. Fun! You ask them to do something and are immediately met with pushback. You begin to feel frustrated. They listened to your shared manager when you were peers, but now that you're in charge, you're met with defensiveness at every turn. One day in a meeting, you ask them to do something and they become combative in front of the whole team and insist they are not going to do what you've asked. At this point, you've had enough. You have a choice: suspend attention and try to let it go, OR hold on to *this* moment, and every one before it, boiling over with frustration about how your friend doesn't respect you as a manager, how it's not fair you have to deal with this situation, how this whole thing is a mistake, how they still owe you $79 from happy hour three months ago, how they did kind of look down on your choice of jeans (sorry, TikTok advice doesn't run my life #skinnyjeansforever) and on and on and on. The latter is what a good friend of mine, Sarah, did in this not-at-all-imaginary situation, and it took her two agonizing months to repair their relationship and move forward.

Managing a former peer or workplace friend can be a fucking nightmare. Emotions, perceptions and reactions can be all over the map. And despite how common this is in the workplace, we're rarely given strategies for dealing with these scenarios. When we start managing a friend, in an effort to jump right in and get to work so it feels less awkward, we often make it way more awkward. *It's totes the same as before, just that I control your salary and career path now. Not weird at all, right?*

This is where the "*story I am telling myself*" framework can be such a helpful tool. Sarah shared with me the frustration she was having over managing her former friend, Kelly, and as we talked through it, Sarah's tension started to dissipate. As we dug deeper into the outcome she wanted, she gradually began to feel more in control of the situation, and at the end, I had her practice a few statements to share with her colleague in their next meeting:

"*When you interrupt me in our team meetings, I feel frustrated. And the story I am telling myself is that you don't have respect for me as a manager.*"

"When you don't do the things I request of you, I feel disappointed. And the story I am telling myself is that you really don't have respect for me as a manager."

*"When you get defensive when I ask you something, I feel concerned. And the story I am telling myself is that I can't count on you as an employee."**

Sarah was feeling a lot of frustration and disappointment, and a lack of respect emerged as a theme alongside her fear of an inability to count on Kelly. Progress! But even after rehearsing these statements, because Sarah had been met with so much defensiveness when talking to Kelly, Sarah was certain sharing any of these three examples would not get her the outcome she wanted. Kelly's refusal to make direct eye contact for eight weeks wasn't instilling confidence in an imminent resolution, either.

*If by the third iteration your story is still NSFW, remove the words "sabotage" and "out to get me." You're trying to find a resolution, not get the other person to punch you in the face.

Wait a second, *What outcome* did *Sarah want?*

It was so uncomfortable for Sarah to see Kelly in the office that she wanted to avoid being there altogether. Her frustration had reached its peak and she didn't see a way out. She was feeling ignored, undervalued, rejected and disrespected. No matter what it would take or what it would mean for her role, Sarah wanted so badly for this whole mess to be over with.

She kept digging. She kept reflecting. She came to me to vent, still very much stuck without a clear path forward. "You're gonna hate me for saying it," I said, "but part of me is wondering what Kelly might be thinking in the situation." She shot me the world's longest eye-roll, took a deep breath, and then the magical power of empathy cast its spell; Sarah had spent so much energy on how frustrated she was—how *right* she was—that she hadn't considered what Kelly might be feeling. What emotions was Kelly dealing with that might be contributing to her behavior?

They had been peers, working together on a lot of projects, on what seemed like a similar career trajectory. Then Sarah was promoted to being the manager of the team while Kelly stayed flat in her role. Now, Kelly's former friend and confidant was evaluating her work, giving her feedback and constructive criticism in areas she had never taken issue with before. This included giving Kelly the side-eye when she'd walk into the office 15 minutes late, apologizing profusely for the traffic but holding a steaming vanilla latte from the coffee shop across the street. The dynamic was different; the relationship had changed.

Anger? Disappointment? Sadness? *Sadness* was it—that's what was fueling the defensiveness. Sarah was sad, too. Maybe they still had something in common?

Sarah decided to put her hypothesis to the test and reached out to Kelly to connect.

"As I've been reflecting on where our relationship is right now," Sarah said, "I feel sad. We were close, and I understand the dynamic is different now, and I feel sad that we're in this bad place in our relationship." Like magic, Sarah saw the hardened expression on Kelly's face soften. Her eyes started to get a bit glassy, and the defenses fell.

"I'm sad, too."

And so began a constructive conversation on how to give each other feedback, how to surface issues or frustrations in the moment so they don't fester, and how to use the "story I'm telling myself" framework to help clarify what was going on in each of their individual realities. And how, if she's stopping for coffee *anyway*, Kelly could pick Sarah up an iced matcha latte with almond milk.

During the entire exchange, Sarah didn't get bulldozed or back down on her desire to be respected as a manager. This conversation was about repairing the relationship, not about winning the argument, a focus on what is often described as "context over the content." Oftentimes in our conversations, we're so wrapped up in getting people to agree with the details, we're blind to the other things that are going on under the surface. Sarah was consumed with her frustrations about Kelly's behavior and lost sight of the fact Kelly was struggling with her own disappointment with not advancing in her career at the rate she wanted to. Kelly was acting out, not recognizing that Sarah was having difficulty figuring out how to assert her new identity as a manager.

In this situation, consider the analogy of an iceberg. Above the waterline is a seemingly harmless structure we can see plainly enough. We think we have a grasp of its size, shape and impact. But when we look below the surface, we find we didn't actually have any sense of scale at all. The thing goes way deeper and has a completely different shape than we realized. When we run into it, the impact it has could be monumentally different than our initial estimations allowed us to believe. Just ask 1997 Leo.

Under the surface, you'll find all of the little details that went into shaping who the other person is, what life events changed them, who praised vs. disrespected them, what they value, what they aspire to be, how they see themselves and more. We all have this stuff—it's what makes us who we are. Fully engaging with someone else's stuff is A LOT to process, and it's a reminder that when we think we have someone all figured out, we're most certainly wrong. People will always surprise you, and what might surprise you most of all is their ability to come around and want to connect once they feel they've been heard.

BUT WHAT IF THEY'RE SUPER WRONG?

As hard as it is to remember, even when you're right, announcing you're right doesn't make you *more right*. This is something I think about a lot when I'm interacting with someone with whom I'm struggling to find common ground. The truth is: being right at the end of an argument isn't an outcome. It's a momentary concession someone else is making to end an uncomfortable conversation, and it rarely leads to the change we were looking for in the first place. You cannot overlook the fact that as tightly as you are holding the conviction in what you think, know or are an expert in, the other person in the conversation is doing the exact same thing.

How do you change your approach to move the conversation forward when nothing you are doing is working? Reframe the outcome from a discussion of right and wrong to one of alignment. I call this framework the "Conflict Crusher," and it goes a little something like this:

*And I'm not talking about agreeing that it's nice outside and we can't wait for the weekend to start. I'm talking, "So can we agree this situation has spiraled into a real shitstorm?"

1) Start the conversation with something you can agree on. To set the trajectory of the conversation on the right path, establish some common ground where you and the other person acknowledge you are approaching the conversation from the same universe.* In most cases, this means starting with the higher order goals or context by establishing "Do we agree on X? Are we both talking about Y?" If the answer is no, then there is more setup work needed to align on why you are talking in the first place.

2) Think about what is important to the other person. This is related to the first principle but goes the extra mile by introducing empathy. Where is this person coming from? What is at stake for them? People are far more likely to change their position when it either benefits them in some way or taps into something important to them. A lot of the time, these feelings sit beneath the waterline (remember our iceberg), and it takes actually LISTENING to the other person to identify them. Listen for the words behind the words. Fear, frustration, self-doubt, disappointment and other uncomfortable feelings are often the deeper motivations behind what someone is asking you to do.

3) Remove emotion and subjectivity from your communication. Yes, it can be hard to do this in the heat of the moment and when you are clouded by the context of the conversation, so I urge you to share your talking points with a trusted peer beforehand and get their honest feedback before you engage in that negotiation or difficult conversation. The book *Crucial Conversations* by Kerry Patterson, Joseph Grenny, Ron McMillan and Al Switzler has a wealth of strategies for communicating with someone in high-stakes situations, especially when there are opposing opinions or points of view and emotions run high. If you're thinking, *Isn't that most conversations at work?* then yep, keep reading. The book suggests sharing the facts of a situation as you interpret them, telling your story and then asking the other person to tell their version of the story. This allows you to separate the facts from the stories, recognizing them as two different things. Stress-testing your talking points with a colleague will ensure the "facts" you're sharing aren't just another story in a "facts costume."

4) Abstain from arguing. Debating is an objective exploration of two opposing points of view. When debating gets personal, it becomes arguing—the conversation stops revolving around facts and principles and people start bringing in emotions or personal details; inevitably, everyone involved gets defensive. Arguing alienates the people in the conversation and IT DOES NOT LEAD TO AGREEMENT, no matter how much you might want it to. When you find yourself feeling agitated or aggravated in an interaction, ask to table the conversation and come back to it later. Take time to mentally and emotionally regroup—remind yourself that this isn't about trying to prove someone wrong. In the midst of a heated conversation, people don't often concede their argument because they've been proven wrong; instead, they usually dig in their heels. Give the conversation some space to breathe and come back when you've had time to cool off.

5) Consider the areas where you are being inflexible and own your responsibility. Make time to self-reflect. Sometimes when we are so completely and positively certain we are right, we forget to consider the other person's experience and context in the scenario—remember Sarah and Kelly? When we're in a disagreement with someone, we forget that from their perspective, they are also right. This is the moment to reflect on your own actions and take responsibility for where you were contributing to the issue at hand.

None of this is to say you have to give up what was important to you or hold back on sharing an important point that needs to be made. The point is to ensure you're approaching every conflict with openness and empathy. It's a bit of a balance, but with this approach, you will often find that difficult conversations are not things we have to run away from but are things that have the power to bring us closer to other people.

SO THEN YOU'RE SAYING *I'M* WRONG?

Most of the strategies I've suggested thus far have a starting premise: You're right. But conflict can also be difficult when we don't want to face the remote possibility that we didn't handle something the best way we could have—that we were wrong. In this situation, the inner critic is like, "Wait for it, wait...for...it.... Yep! You're wrong. You're always wrong. Here we go again." Admitting we got our wires crossed, reacted too quickly or said something we shouldn't have said SUCKS, but the more we practice the tools of suspension of attention, the less frequently we have to do it.

Why is this hard? Because in general, the way we react to something usually revolves around a way bigger issue under the surface than what we're recognizing at that moment. *Fuck you, iceberg!* Are we upset that our colleagues left a mess in the conference room and made us late starting our meeting, or are we actually upset because our colleagues *always* leave a mess and leave it for the women folk to clean up like magical elves? While that passive aggressive Post-it saying "Clean up your mess, your mom doesn't work here!" might feel very attractive in the moment, it doesn't move you closer to resolving the bigger issue: that you feel disrespected. That's where self-awareness comes into play.

Self-awareness is the act of noticing our triggers, our reactions, our behaviors, AND (and...and...and) their impact on the world around us. It's not just noticing *what* pisses us off but *how* we share that information with others. The more we beat ourselves up when we get something wrong, the more we feed our inner critic. And that bitch is like me during 18 months of quarantine: always snacking.

In our story of Sarah and Kelly, Sarah didn't need to beat herself up about where things had gone wrong once she recognized the path forward. She just needed to acknowledge there was more to the story and demonstrate the self-awareness of her own role in the dynamic before she could effectively move forward. The more we distance ourselves from proving to another person that we're right or to our inner critic that we're wrong, the better equipped we are to deal with conflict that naturally will present itself throughout the course of our messy, imperfect and wonderfully complicated lives.

I'm gonna let you in on a little secret: Shitty coworkers are everywhere. Since we have no way to escape them, we have to build our resilience for dealing with them... without the passive aggressive Post-its. As Michelle Obama famously said, "When they go low, we go high." Show up as the person who sees a situation clearly and objectively, the person who understands the multiple perspectives that are present in a conflict. Swap reactivity for empathy, and you'll find there's always a way to get through a challenging conversation and come out unscathed.

BUT I'M A NICE PERSON!

All this talk about proving our righteousness made those conflict avoiders out there think they were off the hook! Turns out, you can both regularly avoid conflict and still somehow find yourself habitually engaged in it—just ask *me*.

Why do so many of us avoid conflict? It *conflicts* with how we perceive ourselves. We're nice, we make people laugh, we are bridge builders. Conflict? Me? Impossible!

In overidentifying with the persona of being empathetic and agreeable, we can start to believe the false narrative that disagreements and feedback (*Can we go one chapter without talking about feedback?* NOPE.) are bad and only serve to hurt people's feelings. We fear that being direct or saying what needs to be said will make other people uncomfortable, so we caveat and hedge and dance around important subjects. Our rational mind knows being direct isn't mean. Our inner critic, however, thinks directness will send people running for the hills—it equates directness with imminent rejection or abandonment, and loudly and overbearingly insists we keep our mouths shut.

A primary reason directness is so hard is the same reason calling Comcast to cancel your cable is such a nightmare: We dread telling someone something they don't want to hear. When we consider "What outcome do I want?" in a feedback conversation, the answer is generally "For that person to smile, listen intently, change their behavior and then leave me the fuck alone." How often does *that* happen? On planet Earth, the actual outcome is that the feedback receiver has questions (ugh), wants to hear specifics (stop) and is likely a tad bit defensive (go away). It sucks. It's uncomfortable. And in keeping alignment with our identity as nice people, we might back down from being direct with an important piece of feedback, saying it's really no big deal after all.*

*Or come away the proud owner of a Starz subscription and a landline when you called to CANCEL your Comcast services.

Connecting back to our tool of empathy, we can be both the nice, thoughtful people we know we are *and* deliver a message with some backbone. We can advocate for ourselves and for the success of the other person—we don't have to see these as mutually exclusive. Considering the other person's fears, concerns, aspirations and goals can help frame our message in a way that acknowledges those perspectives.

Thinking back to the "story I'm telling myself" framework, it's important to remember we cannot control how someone feels as a result of what we say or do. Sure, when we deliver a hard message in a shitty or hostile way, there is a very high chance it will have a negative impact. But in the case of this chapter, I'm talking about over-indexing on the "nice" side in hopes it will erase all possibility of yucky feelings. Getting overly invested in trying to control how someone feels at the expense of having a productive conversation can cause more harm than good.

I, like many people, do not like to see others feeling uncomfortable. Watching shows like *Punk'd* back in the day made me *physically* ill. This avoidance often results in getting walked all over, not asking for what we need in a relationship or buying a car we can't afford. *But the salesperson seemed so disappointed when I started to walk out of the lot!* If you're hypersensitive to or overly invested in not making people uncomfortable,

I'm guessing you have an overactive quality of empathy, and you should feel free to rein that in a bit. Again, consider what outcome you want in a conversation or conflict and determine if you're sacrificing that outcome to avoid a momentary feeling of discomfort on someone else's behalf.

How about this reframe to bring some heat: It's not *nice* to harbor resentment in a relationship or allow a problem at work to fester because you didn't want to have a difficult conversation. That's actually very harmful. Avoiding sharing feedback that someone needs to hear has the potential to hold them back from making strides in their career. Avoiding a disagreement with a colleague stifles the success of a project or team. The actual nice thing to do is to find a way to recognize the multiple perspectives and forces at play as well as the ideal outcomes of all participants and then have a direct conversation.

Love it or hate it, conflict is everywhere. We can't hide from it for long, so we might as well roll up our sleeves and lean into the tools that help us manage it effectively. It might be harder to suspend attention or bring empathy when tensions are high—that's your moment to consider the story you're telling yourself. When it seems attractive to try to prove someone wrong, especially if it's ABUNDANTLY CLEAR they are wrong, bring in the Conflict Crusher framework and take it for a spin. No one expects you to be perfect, but the more self-aware you become, the more you open yourself up to see the many perspectives, possibilities and outcomes that are right there in front of you.

PUTTING IT TO THE TEST

As we talked about in great length in this chapter, taking responsibility can be a BEAST, but it is so crucial to do when we want to resolve a conflict and repair a relationship.

It might not seem like it in the moment when we are upset, but it is shocking how quickly your anger dissipates when you start to see common ground and own your responsibility.

LET'S PRACTICE

Think of a situation in your life with a colleague, family member or friend that is currently unresolved.*

*If nothing comes to mind, then please write a book on how to keep your existence conflict-free, and it will be an international best-seller.

We're going to return to the Conflict Crusher framework by writing a little script for ourselves to help us go back to the conversation with confidence.

WALK THROUGH THE FIVE STEPS:

Step 1) Start with something you can agree on.

Ex: We both care deeply about the success of this project.

Step 2) Think about what is important to the other person.

Ex: This person loves the spotlight and proving they know more than everyone else.

Step 3) Remove emotion and subjectivity from your communication.

~~This person loves the spotlight and proving to everyone that they know more than them.~~

TRY AGAIN :)

Ex: This person has shared they are new to the team and so they really want to demonstrate their value early on.

MUCH BETTER ;)

Step 4) Abstain from arguing.

Ex: [Deep breaths, listen with empathy to where they're coming from]

Step 5) Consider the area where you are being inflexible and own your responsibility.

Ex: I didn't have empathy for their experience as a new team member and felt threatened by their approach. Instead, I can get to know them better, help them feel connected to others on the team and propose how we can form an effective partnership.

That wasn't so bad, was it?

...IF YOU ADD "I DON'T KNOW" TO THE END OF WHAT YOU'RE SAYING, PEOPLE *DON'T KNOW* WHY YOU SPOKE UP AT ALL.

CHAPTER 6

REFRAMING CONFIDENCE

AH, CONFIDENCE. So effortless after a few vodka sodas, so elusive in the conference room. Confidence is something we want most in the world—right up there with more time, money and the ability to make wearing athleisure count as actual exercise.

Confidence signals competence, and often replicates itself: When you believe you can do something, you do it, which gives you more confidence.

On the flip side, competence does not always *result* in confidence, and the struggle for most of us to recognize and celebrate the great work we do dates all the way back to our preteen years. In *Enough As She Is*, author, educator, coach and parenting expert Rachel Simmons discusses the significant drop in confidence women face in their tween years (a.k.a. middle school), only to reach a floor in ninth grade. Research shows high achievement doesn't foster a greater sense of confidence. In fact, the better girls do, the more pressure they feel to keep up with unsustainable standards; they begin worrying one false move could cost them everything, further reinforcing the narrative that they're not good enough.

How many of us were that girl? How many of us felt like no matter how hard we worked, it was never enough, even after hearing our peers, teachers and parents tell us we were doing a great job? How many of us felt conflicted about whether we were working too much or not enough, ready to beat ourselves up no matter which conclusion was true? The contradictions that make it so hard to talk about our work also make it impossible to know when we've gotten something right. Rachel shares that the clinical name for this is "role conflict," or being at odds with the dueling standards girls are expected to live up to. Instead of recognizing it's impossible to live up to these contradictory (and completely subjective) standards, we decide we're the problem and hop on the endless hamster wheel of trying to improve ourselves.*

*Waiter, refill my food pellets, please?

This drive to always want to do better might have served us well in some aspects of our lives, but it sure didn't make for an easy journey. Whether it was to keep studying, make more friends, be skinnier, make the sports team, be prettier, get picked for the role, be the class president; whether pressure came from our parents and families or our own fixation on being "better," I don't know a single woman who didn't spiral into obsessing over one of these traps at some point. For women of color, it's even harder to avoid them.

The Likeability Trap by journalist Alicia Menendez explores the dueling standards, pressures and biases women face in their lives and work that are impossible to live up to, and which chip away at our confidence. Between false stereotypes, systemic racism and the stark reality of only 3 percent representation in C-level jobs, Alicia notes, "Women of color receive regular reminders that their competence is not assumed, their opinion is not held in equally high regard, and that they will always need to prove themselves again and again."

Because women grow up feeling like we aren't good enough while continually comparing ourselves to others, finding our confidence is hard. When we're just starting out in our careers and have to advocate for the work we're doing, the problems we're solving and, most of all, for ourselves, we don't always have the words. This certainly is not because we don't have anything to say. As Meghan Markle famously said, "Women don't need to find a voice, they have a voice, and they need to feel empowered to use it, and people need to be encouraged to listen." To feel empowered to share our ideas and gifts with the world, we must reframe our relationship with confidence.

PURGE PERFECTIONISM

The Confidence Code by journalists Katty Kay and Claire Shipman explores the conundrum of confidence and why we lack it even when we are successful and accomplished in the eyes of others. At the center of this, they say, is perfectionism, a trap women tend to get stuck in more often than men, preventing us from moving on from mistakes and setbacks long after the moment has passed.

My fellow perfectionists and I can spend our lives training to let go just a little bit, to appreciate what we accomplish instead of always looking for a fault. Easier said than done when so many of us grew up in environments where we were praised for being nice, and good, and perfect. After a certain point, we became dependent on that validation, and when we didn't get it, we thought we were to blame.

People-pleasing is my jam—it goes as far back as I can remember. I want people to like me, sorry not sorry, I do. Being a self-aware people-pleaser is a double-edged sword, however, because you *know* when you are doing something for the wrong reasons—to satisfy the needs of someone else often at the expense of your own—which can lead to resentment.

People-pleasing is at the heart of perfectionism, and in *Playing Big*, author Tara Mohr offers tools for how to "unhook from praise and criticism." I knew I was overly attached to criticism (we covered that in our Feedback chapter), but what I hadn't realized until reading Tara's work is I was just as dependent on praise. The two are inherently connected: The desire to please people and a deep-seated fear of disappointing others are two sides of the same shitty coin. Tara explores one common reason for this: survival. For millennia, in the face of a lack of physical and/ or financial safety, women often had to rely on approval- and likeability-seeking tendencies to protect themselves. Considering our history of violence and oppression, it is no wonder we fear going against the grain.

Even in environments where our physical safety is not at risk, the fight-or-flight reaction to potential social rejection still exists in many of us. To combat this impulse, quiet our inner critic and build confidence all at once, Tara challenges us to ask ourselves, "What is more important to me than praise?"* It's a great way to take inventory of the things we

*If your answer is "Even more praise," while I get it, TRY AGAIN.

actually care about when we aren't getting bogged down in pleasing others.

I once led a manager training program that featured a feedback survey at the end of each session. Upon reviewing the results, I discovered I had my very own Survey Troll. He routinely gave my training a one out of five rating each month, claiming the content was useless because he "knew all of it already." The survey wasn't even anonymous! At first, this guy's bullshit hit a nerve, and, needless to say, had me considering canceling the program and never leading another workshop again.*

Then I reflected on the other responses. They were overwhelmingly positive—everyone else said the content was valuable and had a meaningful impact on managing their teams. At that moment, I had a choice. I could let the Survey Troll crush my spirit, or I could focus instead on what was more important to me: helping cultivate better managers. That was more important than praise. Or criticism. And in that, I'd succeeded. And acknowledging that success gave me confidence. So thanks for the feedback, Troll.

*Here are the keys to the kingdom, Steve, since I'm CLEARLY unable to lead a simple training without fucking it up. Grace us with your wisdom.

SAY WHAT YOU MEAN. OR MAYBE NOT. WHATEVER YOU THINK IS BEST...

"I just..." "One idea might be..." "As a suggestion..." Alright, here's the deal: It's time we start flexing our confidence by saying what we mean.

Due to double standards and socializations I've already mentioned (that you've undoubtedly lived with your entire life) and the pressure we put on ourselves to be likable and perfect and keep the peace in a group, we can find ourselves stuck when trying to confidently express our ideas. Express a strong point of view, share a provocative thought or flag a risk, and you'll potentially be labeled "bossy," "irrational" or "whiny."*

*And I don't mean told this in passing, I mean written in your performance review or cited as a reason you're not right for a job.

This causes us to significantly downplay points we want to make; sadly, a worse alternative. Or maybe not. I don't know.... If you think so.

In 2015, columnist Alexandra Petri wrote an opinion piece in *The Washington Post* titled "Famous quotes, the way a woman would have to say them during a meeting." My three faves (in that I hate how accurate they are):

Original quote: *"Give me liberty, or give me death."*
Woman in a Meeting: *"Dave, if I could, I could just—I just really feel like if we had liberty it would be terrific, and the alternative would just be awful, you know? That's just how it strikes me. I don't know."*

Original quote: *"Mr. Gorbachev, tear down this wall!"*
Woman in a Meeting: *"I'm sorry, Mikhail, if I could? Didn't mean to cut you off there. Can we agree that this wall maybe isn't quite doing what it should be doing? Just looking at everything everyone's been saying, it seems like we could consider removing it. Possibly. I don't know, what does the room feel?"*

Original quote: *"The only thing we have to fear is fear itself."*
Woman in a Meeting: *"I have to say—I'm sorry—I have to say this. I don't think we should be as scared of non-fear things as maybe we are? If that makes sense? Sorry, I feel like I'm rambling."*

Are you both laughing and crying? Have you also been a "woman in a meeting"? I'm right there with you. In developing my skills as a coach, I've become more and more aware of how people express their ideas, how the desire to build consensus overshadows the desire to make a strong point and how I've gotten stuck seeking connection over saying something that would further the conversation. In the last chapter, I talked about the fear of being direct. I'm terrified of it. At some point in my life, I internalized the message that being direct is mean and therefore something to avoid at all costs. Unfortunately, this made it hard for me to confidently communicate a strong opinion or direct insight without worrying I was going to upset someone. It was only by being more direct—with curiosity, empathy and a sprinkle of humor leading the way—that I began to build stronger and more meaningful relationships both personally and professionally. I was being myself, and it resonated with people.

Along with reframing our communication, we have to reframe our perspective: sharing ideas with conviction doesn't stifle connection, it fosters it. The ability to build consensus in a group is a superpower, but it must be balanced with owning your expertise, creativity and influence.

One of the worst and most common "woman in a meeting" offenses might be using the word "maybe." As in telling your colleagues, "I was thinking *maybe* this idea could work for our project." What the hell do we think "maybe" buys us? Because I know what it *costs* us:

confidence. It implies we lack certainty, that what we're saying might not matter and we don't feel worthy of taking up the airtime to make an actual point. Saying "maybe" is like apologizing for speaking.*

*You can apologize for forgetting you lit a scented candle at your desk and accidentally setting off the sprinklers in the office, not when someone bumps into you in the hall, and certainly not for talking in a meeting.

In your next few meetings, listen for these "woman in a meeting" moments, where someone ends up diluting their message by throwing a liberal sprinkling of qualifiers into their message. Note the point they are trying to make (if you can ascertain it), paying attention to how brief it is next to all the fluff that didn't need to be included. Consider other ways to build agreement and demonstrate openness to differing opinions besides "maybe" or "I don't know." I hate to tell you, but if you add "I don't know" to the end of what you're saying, people *don't know* why you spoke up at all.

As I said, confidence signals competence. Let's stop downplaying our expertise and reframe how we communicate. Express enthusiasm in your ideas, solicit feedback in a confident way and bring others into the conversation without pushing yourself out. When gearing up to share your next big idea, give this a shot: "I've been working the past few weeks on an idea for this project that I'm excited about. I'd love to get feedback from the group so I can fine-tune it and start running with it, and identify any other partners to collaborate with." Boom. You just brought people along to the party while making it clear it was decidedly *your* party.

MAKE THE CHOICE AND KEEP CHOOSING IT

Working in the corporate world, where many women don't

go long without someone looking at them like they don't know what they're talking about (even when we very much do know what we're talking about), whatever confidence I scraped together in my teens and early twenties had long since dwindled. I don't remember having an issue with public speaking until I started my first corporate job, where I suddenly found myself frozen with fear trying to make a point in front of a group of people and constantly second-guessing myself. Were the stakes too high? Was it my impostor syndrome telling me I wasn't good enough? Was it knowing I was one of a handful of women present at any of my meetings and the men in the room were looking at me wondering why I was sticking around when the coffees and pastries had already been delivered? All of the above? Whatever it was, it took me years to get over.

When this recurring stage fright ultimately convinced me to decline an opportunity to speak in front of a corporate partner about one of my projects—something which would've been an ideal way to gain visibility and advance my career—I knew enough was enough.

Like Rocky Balboa running up those stairs in Philly (or preferably Michael B. Jordan in *Creed*...), I took classes, I practiced, I said yes to every opportunity to speak in front of groups, even if I was scared shitless. And guess what? I started to feel more relaxed, and gradually began to realize this public speaking thing wasn't so bad after all. Better yet, I discovered I was pretty damn good at it. Make no mistake: having built my confidence in public speaking doesn't mean it's suddenly easy or that I don't have to prepare—it just means I don't have to say no, especially when I'm scared. I know I will do what I need to do to be prepared, and I have the confidence to go out and do it. It's as simple as that.

Sometimes we look at confidence and think it's a chicken or an egg situation—what comes first, feeling confident or acting confident? Well, it's not an arbitrary debate. Confident actions *must* come first. This is actually Rule #1 in *The Confidence Gap*, where physician, therapist and speaker Russ Harris examines how to fuel confidence by transforming our relationship with our fears and limiting beliefs. Russ explains, "Each time you practice these skills, it is an action of confidence: an act of relying on yourself. And once you have taken action, over and over, so that you have the skills to get the results you want—then you'll start to notice the feelings of confidence."

Russ reminds us that if we waited to feel fully confident before doing something, we'd wait for eternity. If we listened to the wildly irrational thoughts our Sunday Scaries were telling us, we'd never get out of bed each Monday morning. And if we did manage to get out of bed, we'd be so overcome with doubts and fears about what to eat for breakfast or wear to work we wouldn't be able to leave the house, let alone take on the strategy meeting looming in the distance. Waiting to feel confident is like waiting for your overbearing manager to wake up one morning and stop being an asshole. It's not gonna happen. Reframing confidence isn't about getting rid of fear, it's about doing things despite it.

Given we have to go for it anyway, we have to tune into what matters to us. With public speaking, my choice to say yes—to follow a set of confident actions—eventually fueled a sense of inner confidence. Public speaking connected to my bigger aspirations of helping people reach their full potential in their work, allowing me to push past my fear.

Consider the link between what you care about and the work you do. Don't worry if what you care about isn't obvious to you at first—it isn't for many of us right away. Remember the values and higher purpose we explored in Chapter 4 when we talked about setting meaningful goals. When you think about your work, what are the moments that make you feel amped up with energy? Is it when you talk about team dynamics, work creatively with another person, help someone solve a problem or work independently to answer a question? Exploring these questions can give you insight into areas where you can build your confidence that you should weave into your job wherever or however you can. Get clarity around these and you can shake all sorts of confidence out of the couch cushions.

FACE THE FEAR

Confidence can ebb and flow. A lack of confidence is generally grounded in fear, whether that's a fear of rejection from our social group (no job/no friends), a fear of looking incompetent (impostor syndrome) or a fear of letting people down (perfectionism).

It's time to face those fears and play the "What's the worst that could happen?" game. *Nope. Closing this book and throwing it across the room; I was NOT expecting that.*

Coming to terms with the worst outcome helps put some of our workplace fears into perspective by reframing our "all or nothing" thought patterns. Things like asking a question in a meeting or giving an update in a large presentation will almost definitely *not* cost us our jobs.* But when we bottle up those fears, they become tangled with all the other things our inner critic is wasting our time with.

Even forgetting to attach the attachment in an email?! Depends what was in that attachment... kidding!

Take the fear of giving a presentation in front of a group. First off, here's what not to do: What's the worst that could happen? *I sound nervous and make no sense...in front of everyone.* And if that happens? *I feel super embarrassed and never want to present again.* And if that happens? *People aren't aware of my project, because no one's made them aware of it, and I can't get support behind it.* And if that happens? *My project stops being funded and I lose my job and I move back into my high school bedroom that's currently a sanctuary for my parents' 14 cats.*

When we play the game this way, jumping from one bad thing to the next without assuming we will intervene at any point to course-correct, we convince ourselves the worst case is inevitable. Like, you're seriously going to let all of that shit happen and do *nothing*? Come on!

Let's try this again, with the confidence that if we make a wrong turn, we can get back on track.

Presenting in front of a group: What's the worst that could happen? *I prepare well but I still sound nervous and my points don't come out clearly.* And if that happens? *I will collect feedback from a few people in the audience to understand which points landed and what got lost in the mix.* And if that happens? *I will understand part of my fear is legitimate and part is my inner critic on autopilot. I will also demonstrate I am eager to get better at public speaking and build more of a connection with my audience.* And if that happens? *The next time I speak, I will know the points I need to do more prep on, which will help me have more confidence going into the presentation.* And if that happens? *The next presentation will go so well that a video will be leaked to NBC and I'll be asked to be a guest host on* The Today Show.

Ta-da! It's the catastrophizing "What's the worst that could happen?" game but without a crash and burn ending! You win.

In *The Confidence Code*, Claire and Katty remind us that "gaining confidence means getting outside of your comfort zone, experiencing setbacks, and, with determination, picking yourself up again." When framed in terms of accomplishing our goals or achieving what we want in our careers, there are many times when we fear something and have to do it anyway. Asked to present your work in a large meeting with senior level stakeholders later *this afternoon*? Terrifying? YES! Worthwhile? You bet. Sure, we all wish we had more time to prepare when something important comes up, but if you find yourself heading off a fear by continually trying to buy more time, consider the opportunities stalling might cost you in terms of bringing visibility to your work. And let's be honest, it's often just more time for the inner critic to fill our heads with all of the things that could go wrong. We don't need that shit.

Here's a simple life hack on how to be prepared at a moment's notice to confidently share your work—as you are working, always consider how you would share your project with someone else if you were asked to give an update. This can take some time to build into a habit, and it can feel daunting to plan how you would explain something before the ideas are fully fleshed out. What's the worst that could happen *if you don't do this front-end prep*? Glad you asked: Someone could ask about a project you've been dedicating time and energy to and you might not be able to explain why what you're spending time on matters. Which does not bode well. So get ahead while you can. Having a story ready can help you get buy-in about an idea because you can immediately and confidently communicate why others should get on board.

Having that story on hand also serves to build confidence in our work, especially when we face setbacks or have to defend it. We already know how we are approaching it, what we hope to accomplish and why it matters. This confidence then helps us think creatively when roadblocks arise, acting as our own personal Fab Five to remind us to believe in ourselves. Don't take it from me, take it from Jonathan Van Ness: "You're strong, you're a Kelly Clarkson song, you got this."

Just like the inner critic, fear is something that tends to bubble to the surface whenever we're on the cusp of something new or great. Strengthen the muscle that discerns between the fear stemming from progress or change and the fear that signals you're in actual physical danger and you will find yourself saying "yes" way more than "no." With practice, fear of the unknown will melt away in favor of the excitement that comes from exploring something new.

In *Enough As She Is*, Rachel reminds us that "When girls move through challenges and learn to appreciate their lessons, they come to understand that the outcome doesn't define themselves or their self-worth. They learn they are stronger than they thought. That, in turn, infuses them with motivation to try again."

CELEBRATE THAT SHIT

So often, we jump from one project or goal to the next, barely stopping to recognize our achievements along the way. Sometimes that's all we can do in the short term. But internalizing these wins builds the foundation that confidence sits on top of, meaning if we skip this step, we're only making things harder for ourselves.

As you go about your day and week, in those situations where you have productive conversations or land an important achievement, pay attention to the positive reinforcement you receive. Savor that shit, you earned it! This is not the same as being overly attached to praise. Your successes are worth celebrating. Toast your own greatness.

I know many people who have a folder in their inbox for "thank you" and "congratulations" emails (or even little compliments) that they refer back to when they're in need of a self-esteem boost, and I'm telling you: This is strongly encouraged behavior. In fact, consider it a life hack. These emails remind us that people notice us, appreciate our work and recognize our contributions. If you don't have a file like this already, put this book down and *make one right now!* These can also come in handy when it's performance review time and you need to craft the story about how critical your work was to your company's success.

If you find these moments of recognition are few and far between, fold more of them into your timelines. It can be tempting to not want to celebrate successes until a project is finally over, but mapping out incremental milestones (every 4–6 weeks or so) and celebrating as you go is essential for cultivating confidence in your work. It can actually be dangerous to go too long without measuring success, even when there's more work to be done to get across the finish line. Things can get off track (and they often do) and you don't notice until it's too late because the goal posts were set too far apart.*

When working on a project that lasts longer than three months, establish milestones and checkpoints along the way that signal you're on track to meeting that deadline

*Since when was the client named Linda? Oh, always? Ohhh fuck.

and delivering the goods.

Why is celebrating ourselves important? Because we have to bring more data into our narrative about not being good enough and reframe the story. Like immediately. In *The Confidence Gap*, Russ reminds us that from an evolutionary perspective, our brains are hardwired to look for danger and what could go wrong. With hundreds of millions of years of negative thinking under our belts, these patterns don't just go away after one "good job" email from five months ago. Our brains are thinking: *I was asked to lead a highly ambiguous project = incoming lion = aaaaahhhh RUN AWAY!*

Instead, we must build new habits and patterns to recognize our greatness so that our lack of confidence doesn't create a false sense of danger when there is none. *I have led similar projects and kicked ass at them = fuck off, lion!*

We also celebrate wins to debunk the narrative of "Oh, I could never do that," because by breaking something difficult into digestible chunks and acknowledging when we've met each milestone, we see we *can* do it.

Want to build a habit to speak with more authority in meetings? Instead of starting with the pressure on yourself to solve world peace in one conference call, set a goal to share one question or insight in each meeting you attend. After every meeting, take a minute or two to remind yourself you achieved your goal for that day. Win! And if you said an especially salient point, jot it down right away so you can bring it into your speaking circuit.

With so many forces out there that can shake your confidence, do yourself a favor and invest in those things that build it up. You wouldn't be doing any of this shit if you weren't courageous as hell, so take that bravery into your hands and when you feel it slipping, hold on tight. Stand up and fight for it. Celebrate the wins, be your own cheerleader and advocate, and your relationship with confidence will transform.

PUTTING IT TO THE TEST

Remember: Having confidence doesn't mean we don't have fear, it just means we don't let fear stop us.

Still, lingering fears can cause us to second guess ourselves at every turn, ultimately chipping away at our confidence. So take a few minutes right now to examine your fears, starting the process of dissipating the hold they have over you.

LET'S PRACTICE

Using the model of exploring "What's the worst that could happen?" followed by asking "And if that happens, then what?," map out three of the fears holding you back from getting to the next phase of your career.

Maybe it's managing people, maybe it's taking a new role in another location, maybe it's asking for more autonomy on a project.

Whatever it is, it causes your Sunday Scaries to start around Thursday afternoon of each week, leading to this fear fully taking over any possible moments of enjoyment in your weekend.

Write down the worst that could happen and include the growth/reflection step that you will follow in order to work yourself out of the worst case scenario instead of deeper into it.

Try this exercise each time fear takes over, when you find yourself dumpster diving through last week's excuses for why you can't do something.

There is always another path forward when you reframe.

THE NEED TO
BE NEEDED
IS LIKE THAT
MOUSE YOU GAVE
THAT GODDAMN
COOKIE TO:
IT WILL ALWAYS
ASK FOR MORE.

CHAPTER 7

REFRAMING YOUR VALUE

UNDERSTANDING OUR VALUE is the dragonglass of double-edged swords—first we have to prove our value to ourselves, then we have to prove it to everyone else, but it takes traversing across the Seven Kingdoms to figure out what it is in the first place. Our value is what we bring to the table, the amazing gifts we can share with other people, if only we could put our finger on what those were....

After meeting the inner critic in Chapter 2, you can guess why proving our value to ourselves is so difficult—we're always telling ourselves we're not good enough ("be smarter, prettier, better"). In Chapter 3, we explored all of the double standards that make talking about our impact so hard ("not too smart, not too pretty, not *too* much better"). Hmmm. Then in Chapter 6 we explored how the combination of these factors eats away at our inner confidence, telling us to throw in the towel. Needless to say, we're all sorts of conflicted when it comes to feeling good about where we stand in the world.

In *The Likeability Trap*, Alicia Menendez describes this as "the

Goldilocks Conundrum." She reminds us "what is expected of women (warmth and communality) is perceived to be the opposite of what is required of a leader (ambition and self-reliance). So when a woman acts the way society expects a woman to act, she is told she is not leaderly enough. When a woman acts the way society expects a leader to act, she is told she is not feminine enough. She cannot win."

Let's say you finally do it. You've worked your way to a seat at the table, you handle feedback with grace, you confidently assert your ideas in meetings; you're then met with a new set of hurdles to jump through about *other people's* expectations and assumptions of what you can bring to the table. Proving our value to others requires us to fight against the contradictions, biases and preconceived notions about who we are and what we can achieve AND stop falling into traps that prevent people from experiencing our full potential.

To reframe understanding our value, we have to tackle both sides of the equation: proving our value to ourselves and to others. Let's start with ourselves, because if we don't believe it, how the hell is someone else going to?

FIX THE FIXER

*Why wait to stress about the final exam until the last week of the semester when you could agonize over it for an entire 15 weeks?

I am a serial fixer. It's a cross between a perfectionist and someone who manages their anxiety by taking the concept of "planning ahead" to the extreme.*

We fixers have X-ray vision for messes that need cleaning up, but sadly, we often end up doing such a good job that other people forgot there was a mess in the first place. Over time, I've learned that whenever I jump in and solve a problem for someone else, they are less likely to solve a similar problem themselves the next time. Fixers rationalize this behavior by saying they "just needed to make sure it got done right," or "just needed to set the example for a person to follow for the next time," or "this is the last time" (hint: it's *never* the last time). In the end, we've contributed to a lack of accountability and lack of any sense of responsibility the other person had in doing that task.

In the book *The Subtle Art of Not Giving a F*ck*, author Mark Manson says for fixers, or "saviors" as he calls them, "the hardest thing to do in the world is to stop taking responsibility for other people's problems. They've spent their whole life feeling valued and loved only when they're saving somebody else—so letting go of this need is terrifying to them as well." Being a "savior" is really about *you*, Manson says, not the people you are helping. Reading that blew my mind—here I thought I was performing selfless acts in service of the teams I was working with, and in reality, my instinct to parachute in and save the day was about needing to maintain my identity as a lifesaver. It was about me—ensuring I felt needed.

Where could we possibly have gotten the message to identify with being a fixer? Oh, I don't know...LIFE? From our early upbringing, women are told that our value on this planet is grounded in being caretakers bearing the weight of everyone else's problems, in mothering and nurturing and listening and cleaning up the figurative and literal messes of the boys while they do "real work." And years of practice makes us pretty fucking fantastic problem solvers, so much so that the cycle can seem all too attractive.

Problem-solving gives us an endorphin rush; we can demonstrate our value quickly and efficiently, and for once in our goddamn day, be appreciated. It allows us to put our transferable skills to work, becoming the MacGyver of the office, fixing the photocopier with a nail file while ensuring the strategy negotiation went off without a hitch and everyone's birthdays were celebrated. But it can quickly become a trap that many of us get stuck in because it doesn't allow us to show who we are at a deeper level and, in the worst cases, prevents people from taking responsibility for themselves.

None of this is to say you have to be an asshole when someone asks for help or refuse to jump in when you recognize the need for your skills. In *The Myth of the Nice Girl*, media executive and author Fran Hauser talks about how to lean into the superpower of being "nice" to add currency to your professional and personal relationships (as opposed to letting it get in your way). According to Fran, leaders who are strong as well as kind "use their kindness to inspire their teams, encourage others, and create powerfully positive workplace environments in which their employees thrive because they're happy, engaged, and motivated." What does our niceness unlock in a difficult situation? Where has it been able to build bridges or bring clarity to a complicated issue? This is where the value of "nice" resides. It's about not being a doormat, but being your authentic self and leveraging niceness to maximize your strengths and impact.

And just like with being nice, being the SEAL Team Six of fixing office problems isn't the trap itself, it's how we identify with fixing things as an identity. Instead of limiting ourselves to thinking our only value is in fixing things on behalf of other people, we should embrace the reframe of teaching people how to solve problems for themselves.

FISHING LESSONS

But what if it's faster just to fix everything myself?! Faster for who?

Are you really faster than the 12 other people on your team combined?* I wrote the book on "faster to do it myself," only to find out I was actually just painting myself into a corner of being expected to do everything long after I had taken on too much work to possibly keep up with everything.

*OK, maybe I am...Depends how many cold brews I've had that day.

No matter how easy it seems in the moment to push someone aside, pick up the keyboard and type the email yourself, doing so will cost you more in the long term. If your value is in the expertise you have on handling a particular situation effectively, you only become more valuable the more you teach that to others. Having to do it yourself feeds the "needing to be needed" identity, not the "leader" identity. The need to be needed is like that mouse you gave that goddamn cookie to: It will always ask for more.

A few years ago I was running a large cross-functional program that relied on leveraging volunteers to support the work. If you're wondering how easy it was to mobilize volunteers when everyone was already spread thin with their day jobs, it was exactly as difficult as you're imagining. Virtually impossible. So hard, in fact, that I ended up doing most of the work myself. In anticipation of people falling short on their commitments, I worked mornings, nights and weekends, cramming everything I possibly could before and after my regular hours in order to pick up others' slack. At the time, I didn't mind. This was my program. I was the closest to the work. So what was the problem? I'll start: working an ENTIRE 40 hours extra each week without getting paid more.

Then I went on maternity leave and had no choice but to

step away, handing off my "work baby" to have a real one. To prepare for this, I created a detailed document about my approach to the projects, along with templates, guidelines and resources for folks that were picking up the work while I was out. The result? People rose to the occasion! I have to say, at first I was shocked; then I was impressed. Once I stepped out of the way and gave people tools to operate on their own, they were eager to take on the work.

When you, the fixer, redirect responsibility from others to yourself, you run the risk of solving problems inefficiently while driving yourself into a state of burnout. It's unsustainable. Worse, you reinforce the message to your subconscious that your value is determined by how much work you do, as opposed to the quality of the work or the way you empower others to do it.

When you find yourself elbows deep in the fixer role and need a way out, consider the following questions I'll call the "Fearless Four":

1) What are the core responsibilities of the situation?

2) Where can I uniquely add the most value?

3) What can I delegate?

4) What is the best way to communicate this up front?

Answering these four questions allows you to think about how you want to show up in a given situation *before* you're in too deep. It positions you as a leader instead of a helper, a doer instead of a wait-er and puts you in the driver's seat around setting boundaries. Armed with the answers to these questions, we can strategically deploy our problem-solving skills where they are most needed.

WE CAN DO THIS THE HARD WAY, OR WE CAN DO THIS THE EASY WAY

Understanding our value only gets us so far if we're not able to communicate it to others. Sadly, communicating our value to others is way harder. Saved the best for last.

My friend Max worked his ass off at his job and still suffered from a great deal of impostor syndrome (which, frankly, all of us suffer from at some point). Max was in a a perpetual state of doubt over if he was doing enough or working hard enough, was good enough at his job—typical stuff we women think about relentlessly. Welcome to our club, Max, we've saved you a seat.

Then a new team member was hired, and from the get-go, this person was your typical teacher's pet. When the boss would ask for something to be done for next week, Teacher's Pet would fire off an email within hours to say they'd finished it. After a meeting where everyone had taken notes, they would share a detailed recap. On a slow day without a lot of meetings, Teacher's Pet made a document of best practices to share with the team and on any day that ended in Y, they would create a new spreadsheet to track work that wasn't even for their immediate team.

One day, Max came to me frustrated that this new person kept showing him up and getting all of this work in front of their manager. They didn't leave room for anyone else.

"Is the 'work' this person is doing related to their job?" I asked.

Max didn't understand the question. So I continued.

"We can all generate a lot of *stuff*, but if no one wants it, it doesn't make an ounce of difference."

He was speechless. *It can't be true. They're doing so much work, it can't be for nothing.* Oh, it's true. If I've learned one lesson, it's that the ratio of effort to impact is totally skewed, and in the domain often referred to as "knowledge work," you don't make one extra dime for more effort. Value is not demonstrated through working more. We all work way too much. We all have trouble unplugging. We all go back on the computer after we put our kids to bed. The blue light glasses industry has made a *killing* off how glued we are to our screens. But demonstrating our value has to be about the impact, not the amount of time we spend spinning our wheels and making checklists no one asked for or sending 4,000-word progress report emails on projects that haven't yet begun.

I'm going to let you in on a little secret. To demonstrate our value to our organization, every single thing we do has to satisfy one of two goals—1) making money or 2) helping someone else make money. Oversimplified? Maybe. 100 percent true? Absolutely. We work to get paid, and we get paid because our work generates money for our company in some capacity or another. If writing a dossier of tips and tricks doesn't help others do their job better, you're actually COSTING the company money by sending that extra shit around. What are you doing with your time that *matters*? What did your work yield or help enable? What can you bring to the work that no one else can? Get crystal clear on the answers to those questions and you will start to see your path to success is far less ambiguous than you could've imagined. If you do, however, find yourself questioning the importance or value of your work, there is a good chance (let's call it a 100 percent chance) someone else is questioning it too.* The answer is simple: Remove the question.

*If you've been burning the midnight oil artfully documenting your takeaways from your company's annual report in a document that is longer than the report itself, go ahead and hit the pause button.

IT'S A TRAP

The second thing I asked my friend Max about Teacher's Pet was, "Are they a woman?"

"How did you know!?" he asked in disbelief.

It's not because I'm a psychic. It's because the shield of Teacher's Pet is one I've carried all too many times. And I'm guessing I'm not alone—the effort vs. impact issue plagues a lot of us. Why? When we're trying to make a name for ourselves, we can get stuck rushing to prove our value, thinking we'll get there by just working harder. *If I do more, they will notice me!*

As shitty as it sounds, as the proud mother of hundreds of beautifully designed, carefully curated slide presentations no other human has ever laid eyes on, I assure you it's true. We know how the effort story ends; we've read the last page. We can still be likeable and helpful and all of the qualities that feel authentic to us AND make an impact, we just have to be clear about what we're doing and why it matters.

I don't know the person Max was working with, so I can only guess as far as her motivations were concerned, but I have a theory that's rooted in my own (and thousands of others') experience. Max's colleague was cranking out a lot of work, but the fact that it wasn't related to her day job indicates she wasn't clear about how to add value in her *real* job, so she overcompensated by scheduling all the meetings, taking all the meeting notes and volunteering to chase down a bunch of follow-up items not related to her job.

It can be legitimately terrifying to admit you need guidance, that you struggle with recognizing where or how to add value, that you'd like to seek out additional training for the skills you still need to develop, especially when you are on a new team. But covering up your insecurity by inventing busy work for yourself quickly becomes transparent when you can't deliver on your *actual* work. To make matters worse, women generating busy work reinforces the stereotype that administrative/secretarial duties (notes, meeting invites, etc.) are "women's work." The more we bear the brunt of this (especially voluntarily!), the more we help uphold and perpetuate a stereotype that should've been tossed into the landfill of history ages ago.

Demonstrating our value to others means developing a keen understanding of what is needed in a team, where our skills best support that need and how it advances the agenda of the company (to make money). Again, if it's not clear to you, it sure as hell isn't clear to anyone else.

Max's colleague made two grave mistakes in our example: 1) not being clear on where to focus her time and skills, and 2) picking up random tasks to fill the void. In my experience, it's almost better to do less in a situation where you're unclear than to volunteer for a bunch of shit that gets you pigeon-holed as a helper-outer. "Helping out" is different from helping: its casualness implies undervalued volunteer work, for which your payment is a pat on the back or a high five.[*] As they say with Pringles, "once you pop, the fun doesn't stop;" once you break the seal on being a helper-outer, have fun putting a lid on that reputation.Instead of helping out, you have to help *yourself* and focus.

Focus is about narrowing down, doing fewer total things so that the limited time you have is spent on the *right* things. If everything seems urgent and important (as is with most organizations), you might need to ask for guidance—and that's OK! We prove even more worth by

[*] *And as we know, a high five has about as much monetary value as a limited edition Beanie Baby. What might have been...*

asking for help and then knocking it out of the park the next time. What's more valuable than a colleague that responds positively and proactively to feedback? One that responds well to feedback AND stops sending out random documents! *Too soon?*

If you've tried all of this and you're still stuck, it's time for another experiment.

1) Identify one or two colleagues in a similar role to yours who are successful and respected on your team, and consider what kinds of tasks and responsibilities they are taking on.

2) Reflect on where you are raising your hand for things versus sitting back and waiting. Are these the right moments? Are these the same kinds of things those highly respected people are raising their hands for?

3) Starting small, select one behavior you're doing that isn't serving you (constantly volunteering, working extra hours unprompted, etc.), and turn down the dial a few notches for a few weeks and see what happens. With that extra time you created, turn up the dial on some of the value-generating behaviors you'd like to make more habitual.

The higher you get up the ranks, the more you are expected to work "smarter not harder," so don't kill yourself burning the midnight oil for things you don't know with certainty will have an impact. Value can be subjective, but the things that lack value are often self-evident. When you find yourself possessed by the urge to raise your hand and volunteer for something that might potentially chip away at how people perceive your value, take a deep, calm breath and put your fucking hand down.

STEP AWAY FROM THE LAPTOP

Ah, note taking. How many times have you been in a meeting

where someone inevitably asks, "Who can take notes?" as all eyes dart over to the women in the room? I swear to you, even in a video conference, you can see the eyes of the meeting participants scanning the grid-view for an unassuming woman to volunteer for the job. What the hell is that about?

Not even kidding, in one of my first days starting a new role on a team, I was shadowing a few meetings just to get the lay of the land, and when someone asked for a notetaker, one of the men in the room looked over at me and asked, "Would you mind?" This dude didn't even know if I worked there!

I've started observing this in meetings, restraining myself with every fiber of my being to not just volunteer to do it and silence the awkward song and dance of men in the room hemming and hawing, anxiously waiting for a woman to raise her hand. It doesn't matter if we're volunteering because we're good at note taking! Does not matter. If no one in the room is good at note taking, they can use it as a collective opportunity to develop a new skill. You might later suggest having a rotating notetaker in the interest of *cough* fairness.

As women, we must break the cycle of volunteering for office housework. It is one of the single greatest detriments to showcasing our potential on a team. If you're shifting uncomfortably in your seat, wondering how to turn down someone who needs help, remember to connect to adding value versus just saying "yes" because you feel obligated. In *The Myth of the Nice Girl*, Fran distinguishes the differences between nice and people pleasing, encouraging us to set boundaries for what we will agree to in advance of being asked. This prevents us from reflexively blurting out "I'd love to!" and signing up for the office equivalent of driving a loose acquaintance to the airport in rush hour traffic. Fran says, "It's also critically important to create boundaries at work to help you cut out extraneous tasks so you can focus on the things that matter. Without clear-cut boundaries, it's so easy to get caught up in the minutiae and let important things slide, especially if you're a 'nice girl' who wants to please others by never saying no."

Being labeled as the person who always volunteers for the office chores gets in the way of achieving what we want in our careers. In an effort to be agreeable and helpful, we get pigeonholed into passive roles and tasks, while the people we're taking notes *for* are perceived as strategic leaders, thinkers and collaborators. Getting labeled as the designated notetaker is just as limiting as being designated as the "fixer"; you're pulled into conversations and meetings for the wrong reasons, and you find yourself sinking deeper into the background while others rise to the top.

YOUR MOVE

By now, we're up to speed on what prevents us from being seen as a valuable member of a team. To demonstrate that value and really believe it yourself, it all comes back to strengths and stories.

In Chapter 4, we talked about how getting in touch with your strengths can propel you toward achieving your goals. Your unique combination of strengths is a distinct DNA sequence—no one else has the exact combination you have, and therein lies your value. Supply and demand, my friend! What do you bring to a team that no one else can? Is it your skill of drawing connections between things that seem unrelated at face value? Is it your ease in building relationships? Your undeniable knack for thinking of nicknames for colleagues they actually want to keep? Whatever it is, it adds value.

Next, think about how you can use those strengths to keep a project or team functioning efficiently, or to take it to the next level. This requires examining your team or organization to understand where the gaps are. Do you have a high concentration of team members with one kind of skill set? Are there communication issues regarding roles and responsibilities? Is the workflow organized in a way that would only make sense to a person with a deep understanding of cryptocurrency (a.k.a. no one)? Solving these high leverage problems requires someone with collaboration-oriented instincts.

Remember your narrative, the story of your work and its impact. As we explored in Chapter 3, your narrative has to be centered on the impact you can have on what your organization finds important; the closer you connect your work to that, the clearer your value will be. We can get caught chasing the next "shiny object," always looking for the next big thing to work on, but those are often crowded spaces, and it can be hard to know where to add our own value when so many people are in the mix. If success on your team is measured by the amount of "new things" you worked on, consider all of the ways "new" can manifest, whether that's finding new ways to tackle existing problems, exploring a new market opportunity that was overlooked or creating new lines of transparent communication in order to aid the creation of even more ideas. Whatever maps best to your strengths (and your job description) is the right place to start.

Reframing is all about adopting another perspective; there is always a new way to solve an old problem. Innovators solve familiar problems in a way no one else has considered or tried. YOU are the variable, the unique element that sets the trajectory in another direction. Just like with talking about our work and owning our accomplishments, this is about owning the story about our value and why it matters. Because guess what? YOU MATTER.

So go shout it from the rooftops because the world needs more people like you fighting the good fight.

PUTTING IT TO THE TEST

Expanding on telling the story of our work, we're going to spend this exercise exploring your secret sauce, the special goodness you add to the workplace that makes everything better.

I talked a lot in this chapter about the fixer pitfall because I know it all too well.

Even on our most glorious day where we've fixed all of our team's problems, the "fixing" part isn't where the value came from—the value came from how we approached it. Fixing and problem-solving are two different things, so focus on the "solving" aspect.

LET'S PRACTICE

Think about something you did at work that you are really proud of. It can be anything from hitting a sales or quality goal to launching a product to having a really meaningful conversation with someone to resolving a disagreement; anything at all.

- What about this thing made you proud?
- What specifically did *you* do that could not have happened, or would have taken a different shape, if you had not been there?

Anyone can clean up a mess—but I bet that when you think about it with this framing, you see more than just a mess.

Instead, it was the secret sauce that you brought to it, those qualities that make you special, that was the real contributing factor to your success.

ASKING FOR SOMETHING AND THEN GIVING UP TWO SECONDS INTO AN AWKWARD SILENCE DOESN'T COUNT.

OK, bonus points for trying... but barely.

CHAPTER 8

REFRAMING NEGOTIATING

LET'S TALK NEGOTIATING. Oh, you mean that thing I'm terrible at doing that has cost me tens of thousands of dollars over the course of my career because I wasn't sure how to best represent myself? Yep, that's the one!

I don't have some magic bullet for being the world's best negotiator, but since it's a skill we can utilize in nearly every aspect of our lives, it's high time we built up confidence in our ability to negotiate and *maybe* even get better at it. Up to you. This is a negotiation.

Negotiating effectively requires knowing precisely what you want. This requires a bit of prior planning, but you'll be ready to go since you've already read Chapter 4 on Goals, right? Right. The biggest pitfall I have faced, sadly more than once, was either not realizing I was in a negotiation until it was too late or assuming I'd just wing it. Trying to figure shit out on the fly when you're in a negotiation with money involved is the WORST idea ever, yet it was my exclusive strategy for all salary negotiations before age 30. Patent pending.

When I landed my first big corporate job, I thought I had it made. The offer the company gave me to join was 50 percent more than I was earning in my current job, plus it came with a signing bonus, stock options and relocation expenses. I felt like the red carpet was being rolled out for me, and I would have been an idiot to say "no," so I took it at face value, no pushback or questions. It seemed too good to be true. And it was all good, until I made friends with a no-nonsense, long-time employee who saw my true value.

One day over lunch, compensation came up in conversation, and when I shared what I was making, she burst out laughing. *Jeez*, I thought, *it can't be that bad.* Then she followed the laughter with three words that put my poor negotiation skills into perspective: "You got fucked."

KNOW WHAT YOU'RE WORTH

Looking back on it, my friend was absolutely right—I got fucked. But the sad truth is, getting screwed wasn't something that happened *to* me. I screwed myself. When approaching that first negotiation (if you can even call it that), I did no research, knew nothing about the market rate for my role and made no attempt to advocate for more. And in return, the company decided to give me the zero dollars extra that I asked for.

Knowing what you should be paid requires asking people in similar roles what they are making. It means conducting informational interviews to get a sense of salary and bonus ranges and getting comfortable talking about money. Not discussing your salary or anything related to your paycheck because doing so is taboo is utter bullshit. For women especially, our reluctance to discuss money has only served to ensure we get paid less. And this is in a system where we're *already* only making 54–80 cents on the dollar. It's a scam. Sure, depending on your cultural background and upbringing, you may or may not be gung ho when it comes to talking numbers. But hear me out: You need to know what someone with your level of experience makes in your position, and if you learn other people at your tier are making more than you are, you owe it to yourself to ask for more.*

The thing we need to get out of our heads *immediately* is thinking we will turn people off by negotiating. Negotiation is EXPECTED, and when done tactfully, it is appreciated. Avoiding it demonstrates to people that we don't understand our value enough to advocate for it. If this scares the shit out of you because you were socialized to believe you should take what's offered and not rock the boat, question how that philosophy has served you. Not great? Yeah, didn't think so. You can build up your comfort level by negotiating in smaller ways, with lower stakes things like the price for resold concert tickets or for an extra scoop of chicken in your burrito bowl at Chipotle.*

*And I mean actually more. This isn't The Price Is Right— do not ask for your current salary "plus one dollar."

There are so many societal factors at play, making negotiating that much more of a challenge. We face pressure to be agreeable, to keep our heads down, to not question what's offered to us. Add to that the emotions that come along with the stress: feeling like we're lucky to even be considered (*I'm just happy to be nominated*), fear of losing our chance, being thought of as unreasonable or worst of all, *What if I get it and I can't live up to the expectations?* I hear you. These pressures and concerns are

*Negotiating the price of a used car? Forget it, that's where I draw the line.

ever present, and it's up to us to find clarity even when these forces are telling us to run the other direction. We have to find a way to advocate for ourselves. We've all seen the data on pay disparity, and we know it gets worse when the intersectional element of race is added to the equation. The system has to change, and we need to be pushing on it from the inside. That work starts with getting informed and asking the right questions.

Question 1: What do I want to get from this negotiation? Simple, yet surprisingly easy to miss if you're nervous about heading into a negotiation and want to get it over with quickly. This question is your anchor, what bulletproof argument will you form and what will you research to back it up.

Question 2: What's the top of the range so I can shoot for the stars while still being in the same galaxy? It can be tempting to go all in and ask for something outrageous, like triple what you're making, when you move from one role to the next. *They always say it takes changing jobs to get that big salary boost; why not go for it?* I love the spirit, but when you ask for something outside the realm of reality, at least for women, you risk looking like you have no clue what you're talking about, which tends to result in you being offered less than you might have landed if you asked for something more on target. How do I know? Because I've fallen into this trap, and once you let the cat out of the bag that you're winging it, it's over.

Instead, articulate what you want in the context of your understanding of the range, making it clear that what you bring to the table puts you well within or at the top of that range (and if you're anything like me and have a tendency to undervalue yourself, crank it up a notch and ask for a little more).

DON'T BLOW IT

The example I shared earlier isn't even the worst of my negotiation faux pas. I have fully blown it, multiple times. At one job, I was working as a right-hand to a senior executive, managing strategic presentations, budget, headcount, all the good stuff. About a year in, I got the itch to move home so that I could settle down closer to family. Since I was in great standing with my manager and his entire executive team was distributed all over the world, I figured, why not ask if I could work from a different office? His reply: "Absolutely not." That ended *that* conversation.

A few years later, in a different job, it occurred to me I was stuck in the entry-level hierarchy when I was not, by any stretch of the imagination, doing entry-level work. I asked my manager if I could be considered for a promotion in the next review cycle. "I don't think you know how this works," he said. There was little more to say.

In another role, after indirectly managing a team for a number of months (planning all of their work, coaching them on their career development and setting a record for guaranteeing any tense conversation between two team members always ended in smiles and hugs), when the role of the team lead became available, I raised my hand. Take a wild guess what my manager said next. "You're just not right for the role."

In all of these situations, I muttered something like, "OK, thanks" and hurried away feeling defeated and embarrassed.* I initiated the conversation with no argument and no narrative regarding my work or the impact I was

*STOP SAYING "THANK YOU" TO THE PERSON SCREWING YOU OVER.

making, just a "yes or no" question that could quickly be met with a "no." FAIL.

There was more going on with these conversations beyond my inability to negotiate (including managers I worked closely with giving me absolutely NO benefit of the doubt or opportunity to advance), but that reality reinforces why I should have done more to prepare. Because my inner critic was only halfway sold on me deserving the opportunity in the first place, it was that much easier for my managers to tell me to see myself to the door.

From these examples, you see it's not just about asking—it's about leveraging the right information, offerings and insights to make the case for yourself undeniable.

Between Glassdoor, LinkedIn, a quick Google search and talking openly with your friends or colleagues, you can find out plenty of information to leverage in these conversations, including salary ranges, the amount of experience needed for specific roles or titles and how much to expect from an annual raise. Don't keep yourself in the dark.

Still, for us rule followers out there, even something as simple as asking for nothing more than exactly what you're worth can be tough. Growing up, when I wanted to stay out past my curfew and my parents said "no," I didn't stir the pot—I just went back to my room to finish learning the choreography to the latest Britney video. I've had to let go of immediately caving and/or avoiding the conversation altogether as I've observed time and again how much it holds me back. When we're out in the world, being the sole person responsible for advocating for ourselves, we get nowhere if we take "no" at face value. Let that inner child stay out past midnight and fight for the raise.

BUT I'M UNPROVEN

I get it. You haven't won a Nobel Prize (yet). So what? Does that mean you deserve to be underpaid for your work? Anyone applying for a job or asking for an opportunity is an unproven commodity in many ways. That's some scary shit right there, but there's a secret to overcoming that fear: realizing you're actually not unproven at all.

A 2013 report by Hewlett-Packard discussed the phenomenon of women not applying for jobs unless they have, you guessed it, 100 percent of the qualifications. Meanwhile men feel perfectly fine rolling in resumes in-hand with only 60 percent of the requirements.*

Why do we choose to hamstring ourselves? It's the same song in a different key: We don't want to waste people's time if we're not fully qualified anyway (i.e., being nice and avoiding conflict); we want to respect the qualifications set (i.e., following the rules and not rocking the boat); and we lack the confidence in landing the job because we don't meet all the qualifications (and therefore forget to identify the value we could bring to the role that might not be listed as part of the job requirements).

*Shit, some of them likely apply without any qualifications whatsoever.

This pattern gets turned back around on women, and we're told we just need to "be more confident!" and "advocate for ourselves!" But this ignores the very real part that bias plays in all hiring decisions, which reinforces a hypervigilance among women who feel they need to have *all* of the qualifications when applying for a role (and more!), since the perception and reality is if women do not meet these standards, they will *not* be given the benefit of the doubt.

This bias holds us back and causes us to second-guess putting ourselves out there for opportunities that are *ever so slightly* outside our comfort zone or areas of expertise—opportunities we'd totally crush, by the way. When it comes to negotiating, these same hesitations and doubts prevent us from asking for what we want and deserve. We disqualify ourselves before we even enter into the conversation. So we get stuck. We need a reframe.

A friend of mine once told me about her time in business school and the visible differences in how men and women behaved in class. Every time the professor asked a question, all of the men swiftly raised their hands while only a few of the women's hands joined them. One day, my friend asked a male classmate how he constantly had an answer or something to share. His reply? "Oh, I just put my hand up in the air when the teacher asks a question. I figure I'll think of something if I get called on." Um, WHAT THE ACTUAL FUCK?! Did you just spit out whatever you were drinking in shock, because I literally spit the water across the table into my friend's face when she shared this with me. SPEECHLESS. I could not conceive of raising my hand if I hadn't first figured out what to say (and how to say it, and how it would come off, and if it sounded too know-it-all-y or don't-know-anything-y). *What if I was called on and still hadn't landed on an idea?* I feel viscerally sick thinking about it.

But that dude and presumably all the other dudes in the class were sitting there like, "Yeah, what's the big deal? Whatever, just think of something." WOW. Just…Owen Wilson WOW.

There is a lesson here in *just going for it*. Recognizing there's a double standard, and a greater cost for getting things wrong, we can still seek out moments to put ourselves out there and share our ideas. I'd put money on the fact that those dudes also ask for what they want in negotiations, because they know if they don't put their hand up, they don't get called on.*

Think you're unproven? Says who? When I was earning my coaching certification, on the first day of training, the instructors told us to start calling ourselves coaches. One of the students couldn't get behind it; he asked, "If someone asks me how much experience I have, what do I say, 'four hours?'" *They kind of do have a point,* I thought. "No," said the teacher, "share all of the other experience you have that led you here. All of that counts." Ohhhhh shit, *they got me.* Comb through your experiences to identify your transferable skills, get to know them and start embracing them. These will keep serving you no matter what job you end up in. Start your negotiations on the foundation of the full picture you bring to the table.

When you find yourself going down a path of thinking you are not enough, don't have what it takes, might lack a few qualifications and so on, remember those B-School bros who implicitly believe the universe will provide them with the skills they need as they go. Remember that you can LEARN THEM! The way most of us get better at something is by doing it in context. We can read books and take courses all day, but until we put ourselves out there and try it, we have no idea if we have what it takes or not.

In Chapter 6, we discussed the simple fact that confident actions come before confident feelings. Negotiating evokes all sorts of fears, doubts and stories about not having what it takes. Put your hand up anyway. Remember all the experience that got you where you are and the potential

*" 'You miss 100 percent of the shots you don't take.' —Wayne Gretzky. —Michael Scott."

you bring to the table.

ASSESS YOUR CHIPS

When negotiating, it's critical to understand all the levers at your disposal, creating a new value instead of just offering more money.

Take something like the cost of an apartment. Ramit Sethi, public speaker, consultant and author of *I Will Teach You To Be Rich* appeared on the *Tim Ferriss Show* podcast several years ago talking about all the options available as part of any negotiation. Can you offer a landlord other things besides money to lower the rent, like managing the property, offering a lump sum or maintaining the landscaping? *Ramit said so, why not give it a try*, I thought to myself. The next time I went to rent an apartment, I put his strategies to use.

As is often the case in most big cities, looking for an apartment in San Francisco is an ordeal, everything costs a fortune and I was fed up. But remembering Ramit's advice to look for more levers, I wrote to the property manager asking if I could pay three months' rent in advance in order to have $150 deducted from the cost of rent each month. They went for it!

I used this same strategy in the next apartment, and the landlord went for it again! In the next one—spoiler: I used to move apartments *all the time*—I asked the landlord, and they countered. They offered reduced rent if we took care of the yard so they didn't have to pay their gardener. *Fuck it*, I thought. *I can get a green thumb. Let's do this.* This strategy worked THREE TIMES back to back, saving me thousands of dollars and opening up opportunities for apartments in locations I would have shied away from if I hadn't thrown caution to the wind and given negotiating a shot.

When the stakes are pretty low (like asking for reduced rent in exchange for doing some other maintenance-like service), we have little to lose. In these scenarios, when we ask ourselves that question from Chapter 6, Confidence, "What's the worst that could happen?", the outcome is often pretty tame. Worst case, the landlord says no, the price stays the same and you decide if it's worth it to rent the apartment or not.

When the stakes of "What's the worst that could happen?" get higher, things get more complicated. In a high stakes, long-term impact situation such as a salary negotiation, the worst that could happen is you ask for something unreasonable and they suddenly don't think you're a fit for the company, or you ask for peanuts and receive it, only to feel taken advantage of for years to come.

To fully assess your chips, figure out what you want and what your bottom line is, a.k.a. the lowest number you are comfortable accepting. It's not the number where you've totally given up and given in and feel like a loser collecting each month.

There are many reasons you might go below your bottom line—the job market is down, or you want to get in the door at a company, or you moved into a new career where you're just starting out, or you're reentering the workforce after a long absence. In these cases, consider what you can do to ensure you won't burn out or feel exploited. Ask yourself:

- *Are there skills I can build to set me apart for the next role?*
- *Are there projects I can take on to get that experience boost?*
- *Can I do some networking here to build a group of advocates for my work?*

If the answer to these questions is yes, get the ball rolling. If you're taking something below your bottom line, I've found it helpful to be crystal clear on the why (as in "Why am I agreeing to this shitty pay?") as well as the how (as in "How do I plan to get back above my threshold?"). The answers to these questions remind us that even if something feels like a momentary setback, we can still come out on top.

IS THERE MORE PIE?

Even with all these tools at our disposal, if things in a negotiation get tense or someone isn't giving in right away, we need to learn to stand our ground. Asking for something and then giving up two seconds into an awkward silence doesn't count. OK, bonus points for trying...but barely.

The goal of negotiations is to find the best outcome for all parties involved, and in order for something to be a win-win, both parties have to be...winning. Authors of the bestselling book *Getting to Yes* and members of the Harvard Negotiation Project Roger Fisher and William Ury argue that negotiation does not have to be positional or adversarial. They call their method "principled negotiation" and it includes four points: "1) separate the people from the problem, 2) focus on interests, not positions, 3) invent multiple options looking for mutual gains before deciding what to do and 4) insist that the result be based on some objective standard."

At times, either party in the negotiation can ignore this last step, putting forward something that's only in one's own best interest. Again, this is where being informed becomes a superpower. When you've done the research to determine what would be a fair outcome, know what you are asking for and know your bottom line, you are very clear on the objective standard and can hold the other person to maintaining that standard. If you're surprised by the standard the other person is using, ask them to explain it further—what data or evidence are they using to derive their stance?*

We've talked a lot about negotiating for money, but re-member, negotiation shows up everywhere. Alexandra Carter, law professor, author and long-time professional mediator in high-stakes situations like global peace-keep-ing efforts, offers the metaphor in her book *Ask for More* of thinking of negotiation as steering a kayak. We often think of negotiation as trying to convince someone of something you want, but she argues that in reality, "negotiation is any conversation in which you are steering a relationship." In the same way you work with the other person in a kayak to move the boat forward instead of tipping it over, you can work with the other person in a negotiation to reach an out-come you both want.

*If the evidence sounds like the musings of Ron Burgundy, step away from the negotiation and get a job somewhere else.

Changing lanes on the freeway? That's a negotiation. Telling the hostess at a restaurant that you'd like that table by the window? Another negotiation. Convincing the other person in your shared Lyft that you're not interested in their startup idea but will pay for their half of the ride if they shut the fuck up? Boom, negotiation.

Because things like salary conversations happen so rare-ly, we actually spend the majority of our time negotiating things that have nothing to do with money at all. Steering a relationship requires understanding the goals and moti-vations of all parties involved and listening to both what's being said and what isn't being said.

In relationships, especially romantic ones, we are con-stantly in a state of negotiation to ensure both parties are steering in the same direction, and when things get heated,

it's important to remember there's enough pie for everyone. The third step of *Getting To Yes*'s principled negotiation
technique reminds us to always work to find the mutually
beneficial outcome. For example, "If you fill the dishwasher,
I'll unload it." "I'll admit to having eaten the last of the ice
cream if you admit that you never listen to me." Wait, what?*

Ah, good old "all arguments in relationships," where every argument is actually about something else.

When combined, these two models—principled negotiation plus steering the relationship—work so well because
they focus on looking at a negotiation through the lens of
shared goals. You're reframing into a common perspective
that allows both parties to achieve a win-win outcome. It also
leaves room for airing frustrations, allowing you to re-anchor
to what you value as a unit, void of emotional charge.

Yes, there are some situations when a compromise has to
be made and you both bend a little on the thing you initially
asked for. But when we reframe our definition of what
success looks like, we don't think of these tradeoffs as losing.
Maybe you went to your partner's favorite restaurant for
dinner, but you got to pick the movie to watch after. Maybe
your colleague got to present the important presentation,
but you got to facilitate the Q&A. Maybe you go to your in-
laws' for the holidays, but if they make one fucking comment
about how "tired" you look, you're on the next flight home.

When you know what matters to you, you can assess if
those things are enough for you to come to an agreement. If
they're not, don't just cave and sit there fuming in silence. Say
something. Come back to the table with another offer, discuss
what success looks like as a group and what potential options
might be. If it matters to you, it's worth another try. Where can

you bend, and where can they? We can only answer this question once we have the courage to ask it, and when we do, we open up a whole new set of possibilities and perspectives that weren't there before.

PUTTING IT TO THE TEST

It might be hard to believe based on my previously shared horror stories, but I'm proud to say I've persevered in tough negotiations more than a few times, all because I combined the tools I've been talking about—go for it and ask, bring information to the table and offer something in exchange.

LET'S PRACTICE

With the tools from this chapter in mind, think about an upcoming situation where you will be entering a negotiation. This following process is a distillation of what we've covered in this chapter (you knew it looked familiar!) and is what I call "Score in Four":

Step 1) Do the research: know your worth, what is competitive, what your bottom line is.

Step 2) Just fucking ask for it: literally the full step here. GO.

Step 3) Counter twice: once for money, once for secondary benefits.

Step 4) Bask in your glory. It's kind of fun to get paid more for your greatness, isn't it?

Entering the conversation informed and prepared gives you the confidence to tackle the trickier steps like asking and countering. Knowing your bottom line ensures you don't sell yourself short and reach the counter stage wondering how the fuck you can get back to Step 2 and ask for a do-over. From there, take the leap, open the parachute and glide.

THE
ONLY PERSON
THINKING
ABOUT IF
OTHER PEOPLE
ARE THINKING
ABOUT YOU
IS <u>YOU</u>.

CHAPTER 9

REFRAMING
THE EGO

THIS SHIT IS exhausting, right? Like *all* of the shit we have to navigate on a daily basis? Well, I've got good news and bad news, and neither is going to make this any easier: We have a lot more power than we think. And it starts with acquainting ourselves with our often misunderstood friend, the ego.

Good ol' Oxford English Dictionary (.com because I haven't picked up a physical dictionary since 2001) defines the ego as "a person's sense of self-esteem or self-importance," and in most cases, we simplify this definition to mean "self-importance." The best (worst) part about the ego is that it got its intel from Aristotle, believing the universe revolves around us. It grabs us by the horns, convincing us we're at the center of everyone's thoughts, motivations and wishes AT ALL TIMES.

The reality is we're not. People have way too much other shit to think about, and the only person thinking about if other people are thinking about you is *you.*

Aren't you tired of this line of thinking? It's like that classic pickup line, "Are you tired...from running through people's minds all day?"* Exhausting.

*Works zero percent of the time 100 percent of the time.

You pick up a piece of clothing you wore Monday and agonize about wearing it again the following Thursday: *Will people think I'm a lazy slob? That I literally only have ONE shirt?*

You make a joke that falls flat, and for WEEKS wonder, *Is it too early to show my face again at the office? Because clearly everyone has been laughing for days on end about how not funny I am.*

You ruminate, assuming people are making catastrophic judgments about you, when in fact, they likely forgot about the thing two minutes later. If *you* can't remember what you wore last week, Jerry from Finance has NO fucking clue.

By now, you might be thinking, *Wait a second, the ego sounds a lot like the inner critic!* Why yes, yes it does. The inner critic is a deflated sense of self, whereas the ego is an overinflated sense of self, but the ego can dance right into inner critic land when it doesn't get what it wants. While our inner critic thinks no one sees us, our ego thinks *everyone* sees us. And they're always watching.

Allowing our ego to run wild fuels our inner critic, which eagerly burns up any sense of confidence we had the moment an obstacle gets in the way. We hear a piece of difficult feedback and assume our manager must have been watching us for *months* just waiting for us to get something wrong. When we hear a piece of positive feedback, though, our ego threatens us: "Bitch, you better not ruin this for me."

What got us to this point in the first place?

TL;DR: society. But I'll elaborate for the sake of argument.

Growing up having to consistently meet some unrealistic and unattainable standard gave us a strained relationship with our ego. In always striving to do better, we search for signals to indicate whether we're on the right track, which feeds our ego or the perception we have of ourselves. But because the standards are unattainable, our ego developed an insatiable appetite, fueling the feeling of nothing ever being enough. This is where the inner critic takes the reins.

When we're critical of ourselves, it can be easy to assume others are equally critical of us. Our ego is desperate to see how we measure up, so it starts down a slippery slope of judging other people to make ourselves feel better or more important. Don't believe me? What was your first thought when Jerry from Finance wore that wrinkled-ass polo for a *third* time last week?

This isn't because we're inherently assholes—this is because everything we're surrounded by insists women be compared to other things. Between questions like "Who wore it better?" and the *Daily Mail*'s head-scratching headline from 2015, "March of the Bigfoot Celebs: Why DO so many famous women have such monster feet?," our ego receives the constant message that people never stop considering what we're saying, eating and wearing at all times.

The reality, of course, is that people are not constantly watching us and obsessing over what we are doing. And even in those moments when others are paying attention, it's for an infinitesimal FRACTION of the time they're spending focusing on themselves. So let's take a deep sigh and collectively Let. It. Go.

WAIT, I'M NOT THE CENTER OF THE UNIVERSE?

Reframing our ego helps us remove ourselves from being at the center of every interaction and reminds us that, in fact, everyone is at the center of their own interactions.

Author and public speaker Erica Dhawan explores the emotional impact digital communication has on our ego in her book *Digital Body Language*. With the majority of our interactions happening virtually these days, it's all the more reason to fight the ego's urge to fall into the trap of thinking someone's minimalist reply "K." is a code so cryptic even Dan Brown couldn't crack it.

The smiley face, the exclamation point, the dreaded period after one word. Did Maya send you that curt email because she's secretly trying to sabotage your career, OR is it possible she's rushing to finish her work to get to her daughter's music recital by 3:30 p.m. and is firing off a few last emails before heading out? Not saying I know for sure, but the second option is more likely.* Try to distance yourself from these destructive thoughts for a day or two and see how it feels.

*My guess is See, everyone hates me! DOES NOT end up being the conclusion you come to.

Erica encourages us to slow down when communicating digitally, re-reading the email before hitting reply or removing distractions to fully digest an important message. If our egos are casting judgments by the time we reach the second word of an email, so are everyone else's, and the more present we are when communicating, the better we can ward off miscommunications. If I'm multitasking and responding without thinking, then others are doing the same. Once we realize this, we can build empathy for the person on the other end and interpret "curt" emails less harshly.

Beyond the inbox, recognizing patterns of blame and

judgment in our relationships can also free us from occupying that comfy spot in the center of the universe. In *Nothing Changes Until You Do*, public speaker and author Mike Robbins describes a situation in which he was talking to a mentor about people who were bothering him and things that hadn't been going his way. Finally, his mentor interjects and asks, "Hey, Mike, who's always at the scene of the crime?" *Ouch.* You know where this is going. When we notice we're finding fault with situation after situation, consider not just what but *who* the common element is in each of the stories and where you might play a role. Where are opportunities to look at a situation through a new lens, and where can you take responsibility?

Removing ourselves from the center of an interaction is LIBERATING. It is exhausting to overthink and overplan and over-scrutinize every email and response, always operating from a defensive position. When we get out from under that, we're all just a group of people trying to get something done under deadline as best we can. There are always deep interpersonal dynamics at play and so much going on below the waterline if we think back to our iceberg analogy, but we don't have to run into the sharpest point of the iceberg and let it sink our ship. There is a middle point where we engage in a conversation with empathy, directness and a healthy dose of self-awareness—where we get to the root of the problem and don't get fully consumed in a parallel reality. Let's pair the liberation of our ego with self-reflection, both of which help us see the reality around us more clearly.

IMPOSTOR!

When we allow our ego to occupy a space at the center of the universe, any tendencies toward perfectionism and sensitivities become heightened. And when it comes to trying something new, the ego doubles down on letting our fears and doubts run rampant, constantly reminding us that we should know everything already.

Where does this often manifest? Impostor syndrome, over-inflating the belief that everyone is watching you, waiting for you to fail. For many women and people from underrepresented groups, this is compounded by the fact that many people are *actually* watching you, expecting you to fail.

On one hand, a fear that you've fooled everyone and you're not actually qualified for your job can be alleviated somewhat by recognizing that no one has everything figured out and most of us experience the same fears.

On the other hand, there are plenty of instances where professional women DO have to prove their value over and over, even when they enter a situation where they're highly confident about their ability to do the job well or are an expert in their field. This contradicts the previous paragraph because there is no one answer to the incredibly complex dynamic of how we're perceived at work. For women, impostor syndrome is usually fueled by people looking at us like we don't belong or like we don't know what we're talking about. It's exacerbated by people interrupting us, talking over us or taking credit for our ideas. I didn't have impostor syndrome walking into my first day in tech, but I sure as hell had it later that afternoon.

*Remember me? I'm the one who can't talk about my work without bursting into nervous laughter.

Many of my mentees over the years have asked me how I overcame impostor syndrome. *That's cute. If only it were true.**
I start by telling them I haven't, then share a few tips on what

has tamed it a bit so I can work around it.

When my impostor syndrome is going strong and my ego is telling me everyone is waiting for me to mess up, besides telling it to settle the fuck down, I do three things.

First, I think about the goal or outcome I want so I'm crystal clear on what success looks like in that particular situation, for example, navigating a work meeting. Ego fail #1: When the goal is "for everyone to think I'm smart and confident." When our goals are ego-driven, the stakes are too high and success metrics are too abstract. We also can't control what other people think or feel, which the Survey Troll of Chapter 6 taught me the hard way. Instead, focus on a goal like "reaching a decision." It's clear when you've achieved that, and you didn't put so much pressure on yourself to appear a particular way.

Second, I consider what kind of prep I can do in advance to make achieving that goal more likely. Ego fail #2: When this involves getting a new blazer to wear in the meeting and/or anything around appearance or me-centered validation. Egoless prep involves thinking about the motivations of the people in the meeting, what concerns they might bring that are getting in the way of reaching a decision and how you can connect the dots.

Third, I practice what I will say when I encounter a question I can't answer. Ego fail #3: When your instinct is to close your laptop, stand up and walk out of the room because you've just blown your career in that single meeting. When we're riding the ego train and encounter an unexpected stop, we can be overcome with impostory shame when we can't answer a question. But the truth is, no one knows ALL the answers to all possible questions at all times. Offering something simple and concise such as, "Great question, and I'd love to circle back with my team to make sure we've weighed everyone's perspectives.

I'll check in tomorrow with an update" shows you are thoughtful and want to ensure you reach the right decision. It also keeps you from rattling bullshit off the top of your head (or, in my case, finding your mind so completely blank when someone asks you a question you weren't prepared for that you don't even remember your own name).*

*yeah, I know it's "L" – something, but there's a lot going on, and I can't quite put my finger on it.

Remember, we're not at the center of the universe, and that's a gift. Not letting ourselves get consumed by our false beliefs that everyone is watching and waiting for us to fail is something we can control. And in those situations chock full of bias and double standards, where the spotlight is disproportionately shining in our direction to get it right, we have control over following these three steps and setting ourselves up to come across confident, calm and competent.

NO ONE SAID IT WOULD BE EASY

And then there are those situations of letdown and disappointment where it's not immediately clear to us that our ego is at play. Many years ago, I worked for the Chief of Staff to the head of our department, until my manager left the team and I temporarily filled in for her role. Within weeks, I was far extending her previous responsibilities, getting involved in budget and project strategy in ways this role had not in the past. After a few months, I mustered up the courage to formally ask for the job I'd been covering. It wasn't easy. I felt completely vulnerable and exposed, but the executive, David, had been telling me I was doing a phenomenal job, and all the signals were telling me to go for it. I asked him if he was considering hiring a replacement, and he said he was considering it but hadn't decided what to do. I then asked if I could throw my hat in the ring and be considered, and he said he'd think about it.

Now, I'll admit, this wasn't a great response, but I thought, *Whatever, I'll just keep working harder.* Because remember, "If I just work harder, they will notice me" is tattooed on my brain.

I kept working, building out a new communications strategy, supporting our team's restructuring, traveling internationally with the team and firing on all cylinders. And then, I will never forget it: I was sitting in my office, six months into covering the role, and I heard the unpacking of boxes in the office next to me—the office that my previous manager had once occupied. My heart sank. I walked over to the door and peeked into the office.

"Hi, are you Lia?" said an unfamiliar voice. "Nice to meet you. I'm David's new Chief of Staff and your new manager."

My stomach dropped.

The message was clear as day, and I was destroyed. *And what the actual fuck, right?!*

I cannot express how disappointed I was at that moment. I continued to do the job for another few months, still giving it my all, while looking for the next role that would be my exit strategy. I was heartbroken. I didn't want it to be true.

First the anger: *What an asshole!*

Then the shame: *Was it because I'm not good enough?*

Then the ego: *Why did he do this to me?*

The hard thing about situations like mine is that *why* doesn't always matter. It wasn't me, and I had to move on.

In *Principles*, Ray Dalio, founder of the most successful hedge fund in history and transcendental meditator, offers lessons for dealing with life and work centered on his commitment to a radical acceptance of reality. In his first principle, "Embrace Reality and Deal with It," Ray reminds us "Most people fight seeing what's true when it's not what they want it to be."

Where is this fight coming from? The ego. A radical acceptance of reality reminds us that just because we don't want something to be true, doesn't mean it isn't true.

Many of us have stories of being passed up for a role we could have done with our eyes closed and experienced the pain I went through in that job. And many times, our inner critic beats us up, saying it's because we weren't good enough, or smart enough, or capable enough, or a man... enough. Then our ego piles on, reminding us of all the things we could have done better to have prevented the outcome. But that's not what reality tells us. Reality is actually telling us we're in the wrong situation—not that *we're* wrong. In that moment, reality said it was time to move on, that I was not going to be recognized for my contribution in that role, and I sure as hell wasn't going to support an executive who didn't have the common decency to tell me he was hiring someone for the role I'd been crushing it in for months.*

*To answer the question you're surely dying to know: Was I passed over for a man? Of course I was.

Ray reminds us "the two biggest barriers to good decision making are your ego and your blind spots. Together, they make it difficult for you to objectively see what is true about you and your circumstances and to make the best possible decisions by getting the most out of others." If I hadn't been consumed by my ego, I might have noticed the signals my manager had been sending once I asked about the role. Instead, I waited, built up expectations that then came crashing down when the situation did not meet them.

Accepting reality is hard, but it can be freeing—with a bit of reframing. Releasing ourselves from our ego can be the signal we need to tell us it's time to go, time to blossom, time to fulfill our purpose somewhere else for someone who deserves it.

ARE YOU ASKING THE RIGHT QUESTIONS?

When we encounter a setback, our ego asks all sorts of questions. But are we asking the *right* ones? As children, we ask "why" to dig deeper, to learn more about how something works, to get the details and understand the connective tissue between things. "Why is the sky blue?" "Why is water wet?" "Why is mommy drinking red juice out of her coffee cup at ten in the morning?"*

We get so used to asking "why" questions that we don't learn how destructive they can be in the wrong situation. When we ask a coworker why they fucked something up, it's not said with the same sense of childhood wonder. Trapped in the center of our interaction, something going awry naturally makes it our business, and our ego wants a goddamn explanation.

> *It's cranberry juice, and NO, you can't have any.

Marilee Adams, professor and author of *Change Your Questions, Change Your Life*, teaches the power of transforming the paths that we see available to ourselves lies in changing our questions.

When faced with an obstacle, like navigating a frustrating dynamic with a colleague or having to take on a project we don't want to do or don't feel prepared for, our ego pulls us into what Marilee calls the "Judger Pit," ruminating into a spiral of pointed criticism and doom. The dead giveaway that we're in this pit? All of our questions begin with "why." "Why are they doing this to me?" "Why is this happening to me?" "Why isn't anyone helping me?" All of these questions at their core are a version of the ego's rallying cry: Why me? None of these prompt a breakthrough answer that will pull us out of the pit, mainly because when you're in the pit, there is no answer to a "why" question that isn't defensive. Even a compliment with a "why" falls flat at best: "Interesting idea! Why did you decide to share it?" *Because I'm an idiot? What the fuck does that even mean, Sharon?* Like, how do I answer that question?

"Why me?" thinking keeps us in the judger pit, connecting all possible scenarios and outcomes to something we're implicitly responsible for or involved with. It doesn't allow us to see an objective reality. But there is hope! We can reframe these questions simply by shifting from "why" to "what."

"What else might be at play here?" "What might be another way I can think about this?" "What assumptions am I making?" These questions introduce facts and possibilities, grounding us in reality instead of in the path of an avalanche of hypothetical scenarios that are likely to never happen. That "They're out to get me" shit doesn't get you anywhere. "What" questions help us explore our options and connect to what was actually said, experienced or witnessed. Last but not least, "what" questions remind us that not *everything* is about us.

When David passed me up for the role, I stayed in "Why me?" for a long time. I'm not gonna say years, but I'm not *not* gonna say years. Even when it's hard, even when we're disappointed, reframing "Why me?" to "What did I miss?" or better yet "What can I do differently next time?" allows us to think expansively.

ENTER THE MULTIVERSE

Our ego believes in right and wrong and yearns to be right. In Chapter 5, we explored reframing our agenda of righteousness, especially when we're in a disagreement with someone, and it's worth exploring this further in the context of our ego.

Underneath our need to be right is our ego needing to feel validated in how it sees the world. The more right we are, the more clear and confident we are about our place in the world. Being wrong comes into conflict with our sense of self.

What if I were to tell you that many things can be right all at the same time? Not in an "alternative facts" kind of way (because there *is* fucking global warming), but in a "many ways of looking at the world" kind of way. When we don't have our ego in check, it's impossible to embrace multiple truths—we think it's our way or the highway, we judge the shit out of how everyone is doing their work or living their lives and we are continually let down since the reality is things *can't* always go our way. It sucks, and the longer we stay in this space, the less connected we feel to others.

Alternatively, we can embrace multiple truths, recognizing the perspectives others bring, and not allow a differing opinion to be a sucker punch to the ego. Everyone sees the world through their own lens, perspective and, well, ego, so we might as well acknowledge it.

To appreciate the concept of multiple truths, I like to think of an improv show gone right. Improv pros understand the only way to have a productive scene is to just go with it and see what happens. There is no wrong idea, direction or thought—it's all "Yes, and."

While "No, but" paves the way for the ego to sprinkle in our righteousness, "Yes, and" validates the perspective or experience someone brings to a conversation before offering our own. It works even if we don't like the person! "I hear where you're coming from, and one of the other considerations is…" allows for a conversation to take place instead of a "break a beer bottle and wave it in someone's face" brawl.

Embracing multiple truths acknowledges that many realities coexist at the same time. It allows us to appreciate the differences people bring instead of feeling threatened by them, to see through the noise to the shared human experience, often a deep-seated need for love, safety and belonging.

We cannot thrive in a world where we let our ego reject the perspectives others bring to the table. That starts with letting go of the little things that drive you nuts about your name-dropper colleague, or that one task your manager does incompetently, or the annoying habit your direct report does that you wish they'd stop doing, all of whom would be *totally* fine to work with if they just did things *your way*—take a deep breath and move on.

We need to see and welcome our networks as being made up of whole people who are composed of many experiences, selves and dimensions and don't all work or look at the world the same exact way we do. The beauty is finding the common experience and how we can build a support system despite that and within it.

Reframing our ego requires recognizing the power it has over us, how seeing ourselves at the center of our interactions is causing us to miss out on everything else—especially stuff at the margins. Only then do we realize there is so much more to the self than we thought possible and so much more we can achieve.

PUTTING IT TO THE TEST

I debated going easy on you for the ego exercise, but we're here to work, right?!

In this exercise, we're going to practice embracing multiple truths...it's time for some hard-core reframing.

LET'S PRACTICE

Think back to a time when your ego took hold of you and it was difficult to accept your reality. Maybe it was a breakup, a job loss or a passed-over promotion. I'll demo this with my David situation.

- What was your ego telling you about the situation?

  Ex: David didn't think I was good enough because no one ever gives me a chance.

- What was the consequence of looking at the situation through this lens?

  Ex: I felt bad about being passed up for the job for YEARS. It still stings just thinking about it.

- What is another "truth" that might have been possible in the situation?

  Ex: There was more about the role that was outside of my purview that required a different skill set, and David needed someone to tackle those responsibilities.

- What is the result of looking at this situation through this new lens?

  Ex: I don't feel as shitty. And fine...I realize I'm not at the center of the universe.

Acknowledging this other truth doesn't let David off the hook; he still handled the situation poorly by stringing me along. But it allows me to let go of the anger and resentment I've been carrying, knowing there's likely more to the story.

WHEN YOU REALIZE A MISTAKE WASN'T THAT BIG OF A DEAL... <u>THEN IT WASN'T THAT BIG OF A DEAL.</u>

"Oh well" that shit and walk away.

CHAPTER 10

REFRAMING FAILURE

"FAILURE" IS A word we, as a society, have been taught to fear. From a very young age, right from our introduction to the American letter-grading system, F is the worst possible outcome, which is then reinforced throughout our entire academic careers. In college, grading is sometimes simplified to Pass or Fail, making the "correct" outcome even more explicit. With this ever-present fear of failing, we've developed many strategies to dodge it—we avoid risk and fear making mistakes—while clinging to the ideal of "perfectionism" (remember her?), only to find ourselves stuck in a shame spiral for not taking more risks or trying new things. It's the ultimate catch-22.

There is no shortage of evidence showing us why it might be hard to jump for joy when we mess something up. If we are perfectionists, any mistake, big or small, feels like a failure. We don't give ourselves room to learn and grow. If we're working to meet some unrealistic and unattainable standard, a failure signals we can't cut it. If we've fought against all of the shade the inner critic has been casting and finally muster up the courage to try something, only to fail, the inner critic says, "I told you so." And that feels like shit. Sometimes even worse than not trying at all.

The more afraid we are of trying, the higher the stakes around failure become and the more we feed into the cycle fearing mistakes. The result? We avoid taking risks, muting the creative ideas we could bring to the table (but are just outside of our comfort zone to share). We avoid raising our hands for the opportunities that could propel our career to the next level. Or, worst of all, we actually muster up the courage to step up for a challenge, fail, and then learn firsthand how painful defeat can feel, leading us to fear ever trying again.

I *hate* making mistakes. I hate realizing I could have done something in a better way and didn't notice the opportunity. I mean, you saw how upset I got over that Survey Troll in Chapter 6, and that was just *one* example. For me, mistakes make the inner critic, impostor syndrome, deflated ego and lack of confidence all come together for a big "you're a failure" storm in my mind. At times, I feel so much shame I'd make Brené Brown's research subjects blush.

This is not made any easier by the "broken rung" in the ladder of many workplaces, the phenomenon the LeanIn.Org and McKinsey & Company Women in the Workplace report for 2020 cites as the missing step in women's careers preventing them from rising through the ranks. In a world where there are so few seats at the table, it can feel unsafe to take the bold risks needed to advance our careers, because the cost of mistakes is so high. There (likely) won't be a second chance waiting for us. Pair that with the bias we've discussed regarding people from underrepresented backgrounds facing more scrutiny in the workplace and we've got a recipe for disaster. So yeah, it's a big fucking deal if we mess up.

Sadly, avoiding risks, mistakes and failure only serves to hold us back. The less we put ourselves out there, the less we raise our hands, the less we share the wild but incredible idea that's been burning on the tip of our tongue, the less people get to experience our greatness.

So what do we do? How do we learn to take risks and push the limits of our boundaries? To start, we have to be OK making mistakes. We have to learn from those mistakes in a productive and constructive manner, and then we have to create a culture where we share our mistakes and help others learn from theirs. This reframe took *years* for me to accept, and I'm still early in my journey. But in the moments when I've accepted the obvious truth that we can't possibly get everything right on the first try, I've found myself easing up a bit, letting go of my need to label a mistake as an epic fail or categorize a trivial error as a life-ruining disaster.*

The "startup" mentality of reframing failure into a learning opportunity has helped people begin to understand the fundamental difference between the act of failing and *being a failure*. Failing is an event; being a failure is a choice. But "embrace" failure? "Celebrate" failure? "Fail fast?" The thought alone is ludicrous, until we (that's right) reframe.

MINDSET: THE GIFT THAT KEEPS GIVING

When you make a mistake, what do you think to yourself? Ooh, I'll go first: I'm a failure.

This kind of self-talk is called the fixed mindset.

In *Mindset: The New Psychology of Success*, world-renowned

*So what if I missed my stop on the way to work because I was elbows deep in Candy Crush and had to run seven blocks in the opposite direction, walking into the first meeting of the day 18 minutes late and sweating profusely? I still made it.

psychologist Carol Dweck talks about the power of understanding how our mindsets shape our lives and work. Carol explains how her decades of research have proven that "*the view you adopt for yourself* profoundly affects the way you lead your life. It can determine whether you become the person you want to be and whether you accomplish the things you value." One of the primary signals of our mindset is how we respond when we make a mistake. Fixed mindset is thinking something "is the way it is," or that you "are the way you are." It can serve us well if we've been fed positive reinforcement or have a great deal of inner self-confidence, as it propels people forward against the odds or gives them strength in places where others might back down. It allows people to conclude they are the best no matter how many contrary external signals they receive (meanwhile we're all looking around like "this bitch again?"). This mindset also has its shadow side: an extreme fear of failure and mistakes, because it equates any mistake as a judgment of our entire character. *I failed, therefore I am a failure.*

Growth mindset, on the other hand, is the acknowledgment that we are always evolving, that what is true today does not have to be true tomorrow. It is about believing in the power of our effort, determination and experience. The beauty of the growth mindset is its resilience to overcoming setbacks, making you even *more* likely to overcome the odds and achieve greatness. When we make a mistake, growth mindset asks, "What can I learn from this?" These are the people who walk out of a final exam they tanked and shake it off, eager to go home and study because they now know what to prep for the next time. They're the people who get back on the horse. Dweck reminds us that "the passion for stretching yourself and sticking to it, even (or especially) when it's not going well, is the hallmark of the growth mindset. This is the mindset that allows people to thrive during some of the most challenging times in [their] lives."

It's time we lean into the growth mindset and stop the inner dialogue about being worthless when we make a mistake; it does nothing for us. The protection granted by our instinct to not rock the boat or piss people off has long since expired and we have to break free of it. I'm not suggesting you act recklessly, only that you second-guess your definition of reckless, since it's a subjective concept. Many times, the things that make us say, "Oh I could *never* do that" are actually a lot less out-there than we think.* Start small. Things like raising your hand in a meeting to offer your insight or sending an email to a more senior colleague asking about their career journey are not risks. But even if they were, they are minor risks with potentially major rewards.

*We're talking sharing a five-minute update in the next team meeting, not auditioning for The Voice on national television.

Growth mindset recognizes that mistakes are part of life, and failure is a part of learning. It's not easy to reframe our perspective and look for the "teachable moment" after an epic fail when the automatic response is to jump directly to beating ourselves up (*I'm "teaching" myself to not be so dumb*). But if you think about all of the people you admire who handle failure well and who continue to persevere against all odds, you better believe they are card-carrying members of the growth mindset club. Fast track your reframe from fixed to growth mindset by remembering the question "What can I learn from this?" and you'll be on your way to cutting yourself a little more slack when something goes wrong.

OH WELL

For those of us who like to ruminate, even the simplest

mistake can feel disastrous. Why let something go when you could replay it over and over in your head while lying in bed at night, hoping any sound you hear might be an alien spaceship coming down to rescue you from this shitty, overheated, mistake-obsessed planet? While my rumination habit has been difficult to overcome, there is a simple yet effective tip I learned from *How Women Rise* that helps break the cycle when I find my mind spinning deeper down the rabbit hole. It's called, "Oh well."

Did you ask a question that had already been answered? "Oh well."

Did you get caught spelunking on Zillow during a Zoom meeting and missed when someone asked you a question? "Oh well."

Did you forget to fix that barely noticeable typo in the presentation you shared in front of the entire team? "Oh-fucking-well."

When I first saw my colleague Kim using this strategy in action, I was taken aback. We're so socialized to think our mistakes are bad, we naturally think the mistakes of our colleagues are equally devastating. Kim didn't agree. Kim wasn't going to apologize for taking 30 extra seconds to present her slides on video conference. Kim didn't care that her conference room was double-booked, forcing her to scramble to find a new one after the meeting started. She didn't give a fuck. She just shrugged it off and said, "Oh well." The audacity! Then it occurred to me how much time and energy I was wasting beating myself up about these trivial things, and realized I was the sucker.*

*Having to walk with a group of people down the hall to a new conference room because I got them mixed up? Can we stop at the bathroom on the way so I can throw up from shame first?

"Oh well" is not a free pass to not learn from something, and in these examples, the idea is that you have a pang of "Oh shit," before the "Oh well" kicks in, which motivates you to be a little more careful the next time. Kim's mistakes weren't ones she was making over and over, they were just things that happened, things she learned from rather than lost sleep over. The best part of all was that people on the team viewed Kim as confident, competent and thoughtful— her self-assuredness in what to worry about and what to let go of made others follow suit.

Kids love it, too. Kim shared this tip with her three-year-old daughter, who now says a trusty "Oh well" whenever she makes a simple mistake. Besides picturing a three-year-old saying "Oh well" being the cutest thing imaginable, just think of how much easier things would be for us if we learned all of these tips before the age of 5.

Oh well, we're here now, and that's what matters.

OWN IT TO OVERCOME IT

"Oh well" works well with small mistakes, but what about the ones that potentially cost your company a significant amount of time or money?* For these, bolster "Oh well" with some more meat on its bones, knowing the best thing you can do is own up to it. Ever heard the line, "The cover-up is worse than the crime"? It doesn't just apply to the Watergate scandal. There is nothing that will get you into worse trouble than attempting to hide a mistake and having it go awry. And for the sake of argument, I'll equate cover-up with denying or downplaying something.

*The ones that remind us why we don't send work emails on Friday nights after three glasses of Pinot...

When a mistake has been made, admitting your role in it RIGHT AWAY allows you (and whoever else needs to be enlisted to help) to jump into problem-solving mode to minimize the damage. Doing so in a timely manner allows us to largely avoid the negative fallout.

Several years ago, I took a course on leadership skills where the teacher was an endless well of personal examples that helped drive each point home through his tactful use of vulnerability. In one example, he shared that he used to report to the Chief Financial Officer in a large tech company and was tasked with creating the annual financial report that went to the Board of Directors—pretty high stakes. After working tirelessly into the night to prepare the report for the board meeting the following day, in the wee hours of the morning, he finished. He emailed the completed report to the Board, then sent the document off to the printer for hard copies to be distributed at the meeting before trying to catch a few hours of sleep.

When he woke up, he took one last look at the report. That's when he saw it: The decimal point. The decimal point on one of the profit numbers was in the wrong place—and we're talking about seven, eight, nine figure numbers here. His stomach dropped. His career was finished. His mind raced: *Should I say something? What if they didn't notice? There were other collaborators on the report, maybe they would think someone else made the mistake. The report was so long, maybe they'd just skim through these pages.* He thought and thought and thought...and then knew what he had to do.

He opened an email window and typed out words that he didn't know if, once sent, would change the course of his professional career forever. Paraphrasing here:

Hello Martina—as I reread the report this morning, I found a misplaced decimal point on p. 14 in the profit and loss section. I have corrected the issue in the version attached, and sent a new round off to the printer that will be delivered before the board meeting later this morning. I apologize for making this error and have created a checklist for double-checking the final report in the future to prevent this mistake from happening again.

And the reply? The CFO thanked him for acknowledging the mistake and fixing it right away so that it minimized any impact going into the meeting. She also thanked him for being proactive about refining his process to prevent it from happening again in the future.

When I heard this example in class, I was floored: It's not just about apologizing and admitting fault, that's only half the picture. So many times, we stop there and feel like this unresolved mistake is hanging over our heads, plaguing our managers' minds with how useless we are. The missing link is to show that not only can you own up to a mistake, *you can be better because of it!* Game-changer.

After that class, I immediately adopted this practice into my work and have since been commended many times on my ability to reflect and refine. It completely shifted the frame I had on making mistakes. If the queen of self-criticism and all things rumination can overcome this, so can you. I'll admit, it's always kind of terrifying, and you're always taking a risk when you do it—but not nearly as big a risk as pretending you did nothing wrong or burying your head like an ostrich hoping the forthcoming storm will simply pass you by. When you own up to a mistake through the frame of growth and learning, it takes a real asshole to shut you down.

Acknowledging a mistake makes us human. It makes people want to connect with us. Even as risky as it is for women to make mistakes, I've found the more I own up to something and take responsibility, the more forgiving people are. In *No Rules Rules*, besides talking about Netflix's feedback culture, Netflix founder Reed Hastings shares his strategy to "whisper wins and shout mistakes." Safety in making mistakes starts at the top, and leaders who own up to their mistakes set the tone for cultivating a culture that views mistakes as lessons rather than failures.

If you don't feel safe "shouting mistakes" yet, that's OK. Stress-test the incident with a few trusted peers, and ask: Who determined something is/was a mistake? Did the work still get done? How many people (or how much money) were impacted based on your mistake?

Tap into your squad of people who you can learn with, who you can share failures and laugh with, the people who will be there for you even if you call your boss's boss the wrong name. These are the people who will help you discern whether something is an earth-shattering mistake or just an "Oh well." I guarantee there are fewer egregious mistakes in your work than you're giving yourself credit for. When you realize a mistake wasn't that big of a deal...THEN IT WASN'T THAT BIG OF A DEAL. "Oh well" that shit and walk away.

SELF-REFLECTION IS A SUPERSTRENGTH

Reflecting on our own is one thing; it can feel a little dicier when owning up to a mistake or failure in front of a team. To put some structure around this, many companies and teams like to host post-mortems or retrospectives following the completion of a project, meetings where people examine what went well and what could be improved for the next time. These can help create a more open culture around feedback and levity when it comes to talking about mistakes, both recognizing the positives and areas of improvement, so that the focus isn't only on what went wrong.

In one of the best versions of these that I attended, we sat in a circle and went around three times, with each person sharing a short example. We didn't hold hands, but it still had a strong summer camp vibe.

Round 1 was about sharing what went well. We got all of the high-fives and pats on the backs out of the way, beginning the meeting in celebration of what we had accomplished.

Round 2 was about sharing what could've gone better. This round focused on the thing we observed that didn't quite land right or that made the road to completing the project harder than it needed to be.

Round 3 was the secret sauce and the real hidden purpose of the whole meeting. This round is about saying what you *personally* will do differently next time. YOU is the operative word here, because that is who you have control over.

Round 3 is the trickiest and most uncomfortable. In the spirit of "Oh well" and taking responsibility for something that didn't quite go as planned, this step is critical. I've seen people sneakily try to bypass Round 3 and just give another Round 2 example, but when this happens, they miss out on the learning.

When we make a mistake, there is inevitably something we could have done differently. Kinda obvious, right? And when a series of mistakes compound together to lead to a larger failure, it's even more so the case. If we're not willing to acknowledge our role in something, we're doomed to repeat it.

Acknowledging our role isn't about shaming ourselves or beating ourselves up, it's about demonstrating our capacity to grow and learn. It doesn't mean we say to our team, "I'm a loser and always mess things up." Not only does that make people super uncomfortable (*looks like she's really got some shit to work through*), but it doesn't demonstrate what will be different the next time around. In fact, with that attitude, it's likely the next time will look frighteningly similar, because your fixed mindset is talking, saying you're a permanent loser. Instead, let self-reflection take the reins and say something like, "Thinking back on the process, I made the call early on to start the project without completing the research phase. We were pressed for time, and it seemed like we had enough insight to go on, but looking back, I see that it led us to a conclusion we wouldn't have made if we'd been fully informed. Next time, I will ensure we complete this step." Does that sound like "I'm a loser"? No! It sounds like a person who is thoughtful and reflective and can take responsibility.

WHAT DO YOU NEED?

I was once on a team where I worked with a fantastic designer who out of nowhere started missing his deadlines. To add to this, I'd look over at his desk, and he'd seemingly be standing around looking lost for long periods of time. His manager and I began to get worried. Was he unhappy on the team and looking for a new role? Could he not handle his workload? After he missed another deadline, I went and asked him about it.

"Hey Evan, you're doing awesome work, but we just missed a huge deadline, and I wanted to see if there was anything I can help with to get the project back on track."*

"Yes, thank you for coming to talk to me. My computer has a virus on it and keeps crashing, losing all of my saved work. Can you help me order a new computer?"

COME ON, DUDE! WHY DIDN'T YOU SAY SOME-THING?! Evan explained that he had ordered a new

*Spoiler: "Help me help you" is project manager code for "Get the fuck back to work."

computer but the expense was rejected (corporate bureau-
cracy for the win), so he took it upon himself to just muscle
through using his broken one. I figured out how to override
the approvals so he could get a new computer (Fixer for the
win) and not surprisingly, Evan was soon back up and running at his old pace. But my conversation with Evan put a
spotlight on an issue many of us have when it comes to failure: not asking for what we need to prevent one to begin with.

Asking for something is hard, especially when you are in
an environment where the answer is generally "no." But as
we covered in our Negotiation chapter, are you asking in the
right way? When something is legitimately preventing you
from doing your job well, you've got to escalate it. Otherwise
people start making all sorts of judgments about you. Here
we were, starting to jump to the conclusion that Evan's work
ethic was the problem, when it was just an equipment issue.* When asking for something, describe the issue objectively and provide solutions or ideas instead of just dropping
a problem on someone's lap. This allows the person to hear
us out rather than cast judgments and assume we're unable
to "handle" something. A quick framework to try:

> *Honestly,
> dude, when were
> you going to say
> something?*

Describe the situation: "Right now, I am allocated
across 14 projects."

Describe the problem: "I am working 12-hour days in
order to get everything done, and when a stakeholder has
a last-minute request that has to be prioritized, some of my
projects don't get done."

Describe the proposal: "I'm seeing two potential
routes, having a reset conversation with our stakeholders

to renegotiate priorities, or asking for the budget to hire a temp to offload some of the work."

The key to this framework is that it's used *before* an issue turns into a mistake or failure. It's all about risk mitigation. Yes, I'll be the first to say it: It's also about covering your ass so if you aren't able to get support for the problem you addressed, you've already let people know what the risks are. And yeah, we do have to do some ass-covering from time to time. But more than that, this approach allows us to distance ourselves from assuming the pressure of having to take on something we know is going to fail, as we've already acknowledged the issues that are dooming it in the first place. It allows you to set some boundaries and let go.

In the end, reframing failure is all about self-reflection, and this is no easy feat. It gets harder the more we care about something or the more emboldened we are about a situation. The more we practice it, the more we can take responsibility for our mistakes, accept ourselves as whole people and forge a path of continual growth. We have to let go of the false sense that there's a "perfect" out there we can attain *if we just* (fill in the blank). There isn't. Not only is perfection an illusion, but the concept is so subjective that you might be working to realize a vision of perfection that is not the same in the person's eyes you're striving so hard to please.

Recognizing that making a mistake does not make you a failure opens up the door for you to take more risks, try more things and ask for what you want. In doing so, you become a better version of yourself.

We can't get stuck in being both too proud and too ashamed to make mistakes. Lean toward the growth mindset and the acceptance of "Oh well," share what you will do differently in the future, ask for help when you need it and you will be so much further ahead than those who continue to dig their heels in deeper. This behavior is as refreshing as it is transformational. Give it a try. Start with situations and peers who are safe to test the waters with. Get feedback. I promise you, there will be something to gain.

PUTTING IT TO THE TEST

It's a lot easier to read and nod your head in agreement about owning up to mistakes than to actually do it.

As a recovering perfectionist, the more I started to talk about where I made a mistake with humility, along with what I learned from the experience and what I will do differently next time, the more liberated I felt from the hold the mistake had over me.

LET'S PRACTICE

Think back to a mistake you made that is still fresh, hasn't quite scabbed over yet. The cringier, the better.

CONSIDER THE FOLLOWING QUESTIONS:

1) What happened?

2) Who do you need to come clean to, apologize to, etc. about the mistake?

3) What have you learned from this mistake?

4) How have you changed your process to avoid this mistake in the future?

5) NEW STEP! Is there still time to course correct and fix the mistake?

If the answer to question number five is "yes," then put down this book, grab your cheat sheet of answers and GO FIX IT.

SUGGEST SOMEONE BE RESPONSIBLE FOR SOMETHING, AND THE IMAGE OF A NAGGING MOM IS IMMEDIATELY CHANNELED.

CHAPTER 11

REFRAMING ACCOUNTABILITY

WHEN I TELL people "accountability" is my favorite word in the English language, their reaction is something between being totally horrified and wanting to have nothing to do with me—I mean, I *did* write an entire book about it (yes, my "I WROTE A BOOK" book from Chapter 3). Ironically, it's the same reaction you'll get if you ask people to be accountable for something in the workplace.

Why is this? Why are we so averse to the term "accountability," for taking on the responsibility of getting something done?

Accountability can elicit feelings of shame, blame or even retribution. There are no positive connotations with the word "blame"—you get those deep, uncomfortable sighs or eye rolls I mentioned every time I bring it up.* Saying the word makes people feel like they're in trouble or did something wrong. It's also abstract. It feels systemic,

*"*Great job on this project! Who can I blame for this?*" doesn't quite have the right ring to it, does it?

like ending world hunger. "Hold your organization accountable." *Cool, yeah, I'll get right on that. How do I do it? What do you want from me?!*

In *The Gifts of Imperfection*, Brené Brown recognizes why this isn't easy. "We live in a blame culture—we want to know whose fault it is and how they're going to pay," she writes. We can get stuck in this pattern—it's hard to do and takes work, we don't quite know what we're asking someone for, it's easier in the moment to vent and go back to fixing, you name it. But when we are stuck in this loop, our requests are ignored or dismissed, fueling a cycle of our needs going unmet in a society that *already* tends to take the requests of men more seriously.

Think about the interesting link between the words "accountability" and "responsibility." While there are many instances where the words are synonymous, people don't tend to be averse to being responsible or taking responsibility for something. The nuance between the two words is the *who*—while many people can be responsible for something, only ONE person can truly be held accountable. This makes accountability very lonely.

We have to stop getting stuck in the trap of seeing accountability as blame. If we instead start viewing accountability through the lens of "ownership," i.e., taking responsibility for seeing something through, we can reframe the word into a safe zone and begin to think in terms of credit as opposed to blame. We can then use that credit to reward and recognize (as opposed to punish) someone.

Take a basic example like renting vs. owning a home. When you rent an apartment and you have a leaky faucet, you call the landlord and they are on the hook for sending someone over to fix it. They might hire the cheapest person possible (or their non-plumber friend who ends up half-assing the job), but they send someone and they pay for the labor. In this scenario, sure, you care about the apartment, you want it to be kept in good condition, but the responsibility to make major repairs lies with the owner, not you.

Owning a home is a whole new ballgame. When the plumbing breaks because you used too much toilet paper (even though your parents taught you better), tough luck. It is 100 percent YOUR problem now. You have to find the repair company, you have to meet them at the house and, of course, you have to pay them. You also have to sit there as they snake hair out of the shower drain and look at you in disgust after you said "not sure what happened" when they asked how the drain got clogged. If you are too busy to call the plumber, can't afford their services or feel like it's someone else's problem to solve, the plumber doesn't come and the issue doesn't get fixed. Because you've committed to ownership of the house, you're responsible for it whether things are going well or not.

Similarly, owning something at work means being on the hook for it from a time, cost and responsibility standpoint. Yet when we're faced with owning an outcome, more often than not, in environments striving to be collaborative and give credit to all people involved in solving a problem, we avoid putting one person's name on the line for a task. We shuffle our feet when it's time to step up to the plate and have difficulty taking ownership—likely because we don't want to be left with the career equivalent of an overflowing toilet. But sadly, it's the *avoidance* of accountability that will leave you alone in the middle of the night with the plunger in hand. If you don't find the rightful owner, you're bound to get stuck with the task.

ACCOUNTABILITY ISN'T ANGRY, IT'S DISAPPOINTED

I once worked with a manager, Cindy, who struggled a lot with holding people accountable. In her organization, Cindy was someone people would describe as a "team player," someone team members looked up to for optimism and positivity, who felt more comfortable congratulating as opposed to delivering hard feedback. Cindy wanted to demonstrate that she trusted her managers and team members to make the right decisions, and she believed good behavior was best achieved through positive reinforcement. All great things, except there were no structures in place for what to do when something went wrong or people didn't agree. No one saw the need to put themselves on the line for a decision.

In her desire to be "nice," Cindy fell into one of the behaviors that leads to ineffectiveness on teams, according to *The Five Dysfunctions of a Team* by world-class business consultant Patrick Lencioni: you guessed it, "Avoidance of Accountability." When teams have an avoidance of accountability, Patrick explains, it is often directly tied to the leader feeling uncomfortable being direct with their team. In a world where we associate accountability with blame, it's no wonder Cindy avoids it altogether. She thinks holding people accountable makes her an asshole. But we know better. Let's reframe.

If Cindy were to look deeper, she would realize it's not the act itself, but her interpretation—the baggage she has given the word—that makes her want to distance herself from holding people accountable. When our definition of accountability is the act of owning responsibility, it's something a leader of an organization can find more comfort with—they have to if they want any shot at inspiring and motivating their team.

As a people pleaser, I've struggled with this. I talk a big game about accountability, but it doesn't mean it's easy for me to ask it of others. I honor the commitments I make and am a machine when it comes to follow-through—I am proud to own those aspects of my work ethic. But as we explored in Chapter 7, this same work ethic can lead to a slippery slope of "just doing everything myself," and I've had to become more comfortable raising awareness of the commitments *others* have made, too, especially when they've fallen behind.

Asking someone about that *thing* they committed to that they *didn't do* is by no means a fun conversation to have. For women, it can be even more daunting. We are expected to be consensus builders, accommodating and collaborative by nature. As Sheryl Sandberg pointed out a long time ago, when we try to hold people accountable, we're called BOSSY! Suddenly, we're aggressive, overstepping, emotional; we seem upset, unapproachable, standoffish, and the list goes on. Yet what happens when we accommodate? Does it get any easier? HELL NO—now we're told we're not authoritative, or leaders, or assertive enough. These double standards impact women of color more significantly and in ways that are more detrimental. The irony in the difficulty of women holding people accountable is that because of our socialization to be more collaborative and observant, women more often identify the situations where accountability is lacking. So here we are, knowing full well there is a pervasive problem, and when we raise the issue, we are told to get back in our seats. Thanks, fellas.

The garbage we tell women—high achieving, star performer women—is freakin' bananas. It's no wonder we think twice before we toss the word accountability around. Suggest someone be responsible for something, and the image of a nagging mom is immediately channeled.

I'm not angry, I'm disappointed.

Too soon?

In *Becoming*, Michelle Obama's memoir of her journey into adulthood, being the First Lady and beyond, she reminds us, "The easiest way to disregard a woman's voice is to package her as a scold." Pop culture only reinforces this. Countless sitcoms on TV bolster the stereotype of a wife nagging her husband to do something while he sits on the sofa drinking beer and watching the game, completely ignoring her. And *he's* the hero! Even if we are a wife or think the wife character made a good point, we empathize with the husband because he's typically the comic relief. *Give the guy a break*, we think, *he had a hard day at work.****

*To all the TV wives out there, we see you. We see you and those toned-ass arms of yours.

We want to be leaders, not nags. We want to hold people accountable, not scold.

In the book *Burnout*, educators and twin sisters Emily and Amelia Nagoski call this phenomenon the "Human Giver Syndrome," or the "deeply buried, unspoken assumption that women should give everything, every moment of their lives, every drop of energy, to the care of others." We're expected to be in continual service to other people, to not make too much of a fuss when things go wrong, to be flexible, gracious and accommodating but also eagle-eyed, ensuring nothing falls through the cracks.***

*It's the literal manifestation of The Giving Tree where the boy takes and takes and takes until the tree (a she) goes from being a beautiful flourishing tree to a weathered, worn-out stump.

We start taking the job to heart, inadvertently holding ourselves accountable for the responsibilities of others. Whoops. We get stuck carrying the weight of everything we have to worry about, along with all the things our team members (and likely family members) have to worry about, with no room to get any space for ourselves. The result? More work *and* a degraded sense of well-being. And when we follow a path of giving and giving with very little in return, we're led to only one destination: burnout.

A PATH TO BURNOUT

Burnout hits when we're overextended and don't see a way through, the natural consequence of feeling responsible for everything and carrying the endless weight of everyone else's stress without assigning it back to the rightful owner. Burnout is similar to stress, but while stress is associated with physiological symptoms (e.g., stomach ache, raised blood pressure), burnout is associated with psychological symptoms (e.g., depression, hopelessness). The concept of grit, of being resilient to whatever is thrown our way—and of hustle culture in general—often snowballs into burnout, because after volleying stressful situations back and forth so many times, we tend to not realize when we've reached our max.

In *Burnout*, Emily and Amelia discuss the importance of distinguishing between the stressors and the stress response that leads to burnout so that we're not left charged up and out of balance long after the stress is gone. When we're in a heightened state of stress, our body doesn't shift to calm the moment the stressor goes away. We have to complete the "stress response cycle," which could mean taking a walk, yelling into a pillow, laughing: whatever it takes to decompress after the situation. We can't get over burnout if we persist as a pot boiling over at all times—that's a recipe for disaster.

Let's start by recognizing the stressors. For me, the most reliable indicator of burnout is when I feel like I'm the only one taking ownership over risks in a project, the only one taking on the leftover work people didn't want to pick up. I feel burnout when I have to convince others to step up to the plate, like I'm walking uphill on a treadmill that has no end and where no calories are burned (#wasteoftime). I feel burnout when I witness people saying they want something to happen, that they expect it to happen while doing absolutely nothing to kick that goal into action, as if saying "Let's do it!" is all that's required to achieve a monumental task. Each of these stressors, when built up, completely kill my motivation over time.

My greatest stress response cycle completion activity, far beyond doing some deep breathing and taking a jog, is helping people find accountability.[*]

*Hell yeah that relieves stress for me. You want to go on a 3-mile run, I want to hold some team members accountable to finishing those TPS reports. Tomato, to-mah-to.

When all of the reasons that cause my burnout are directly related to a lack of ownership, starting there is the only way to release its hold. Unfortunately, turning around and saying "no" to everything doesn't help me feel any better. In an attempt to have my cake and eat it too, I've developed the following strategy to hold people accountable and *still* say yes! I call it "Free in Three."

Imagine you observe a situation that would benefit greatly from your expertise, but you want to make sure you don't get stuck with the plunger. It's time to say "yes" and renegotiate the terms. Let's use the example of hiring a new team member.

Set the terms: Be specific about what you will do, ensuring it lines up to the bigger story of how you add value in your organization.

Ex: Outline the responsibilities and key projects for the role. Bonus: This allows me to demonstrate my vision for the direction of the team.

Enlist others: Discuss what additional resources are needed to cover the work outside of your scope.

Ex: Three additional team members to meet with candidates

Set boundaries: Be clear on what you will work on when based on the full picture of your workload.

Ex: Write the job description this week and then meet two candidates per week starting next month.

Establishing accountability doesn't mean throwing things over the fence, being disagreeable or saying "no" to opportunities you actually want. It's about finding the *right* owner at the *right* time for the *right* set of tasks. When I'm burned out, I can no longer determine what I have the capacity for because everything extra just feels like too much. Doing this exercise and setting boundaries allows us to reach and explore without getting overwhelmed, knowing we've set clear limits.

GREAT EXPECTATIONS

Earlier in the chapter, we met a manager, Cindy, who in her eagerness to build connection with her team let accountability fall by the wayside. Cindy wanted to be liked and respected and hoped everyone would take as much pride in their work and in honoring their commitments as she did. What she didn't account for is that a team might have their own set of motivations and priorities that could be out of sync with hers. But alas, no one says anything, until Cindy gets fed up one day and sends an email claiming to be disappointed that something she never asked for didn't happen. Now, she *is* an asshole!

No one wins in this example.

What Cindy was missing in her effort to be Ms. Nice Boss was the accountability-centered act of setting expectations. It's kind of the most non-asshole thing you can do for people. In *The Gifts of Imperfection,* Brené reminds us that without accountability, we can feel resentment when people can't read our minds, essentially "priming ourselves for the shame and blame game."

The irony in all of this is people are actually drawn to ownership and clear expectations. They crave it. We get comfort in knowing what belongs to us, what we can call our own, what we can point to as our success. It forges a greater sense of connection because we see someone is invested in us. As leaders, the less we fear accountability, the more we can create a culture around it.

Across the countless projects and deliverables I've overseen over the years, there are always those people who seem tough to pin down. Sometimes this gives others the impression they're off on tangents or are unreliable. But I always find the opposite to be true. My secret? Talking to them.

When faced with a person who seems to be avoiding ownership, I sit down with them to discuss what support they need in order to be successful. I help them map out the work and their next steps of action so they can move forward. I often stay with them for a bit, talking through the challenges they've had, the frustrations they've encountered and whether it's with the work or their stakeholders. Mostly, I listen to them.

Each time I try this approach, not only does the person deliver on the work they committed to, but they start including me on emails where they're handing in their deliverables. They literally create an accountability chain *for themselves*! The root of the issue was never that they were unable to follow timelines, but that no one was listening to them about what obstacles were in their way or caring if they delivered on something or not. The people assigning the work were not taking responsibility over *their* ownership; they threw the work over the fence assuming it would get done without providing any context or information.

This boils down to expectation-setting. It means not just dropping work on someone's lap and returning when you think it should be ready but being clear about what you are looking for and what is realistic.

Expectation-setting is an absolutely critical step, yet so many times we gloss right over it. We think, *I told someone to do something, what's the problem? I emailed them, and they didn't respond. It's their problem now.* Does anyone really believe this?

I once worked with a designer named Alex who was incredibly smart and talented but was late on finishing many of their deliverables week after week. While collaborating on a project, I got a chance to get visibility into their work and, as I suspected, Alex's pace was not due to a lack of ability, caring, rigor or whatever negative conclusion others had drawn. Although I only relied on Alex for a few deliverables, I sat down with them and walked through all of their work, stack ranking everything into a prioritized list. We talked about what they could get done right away, what they needed more information on and what was assigned to them blindly that wasn't even their responsibility to work on. For the set of tasks they could get done right away, they knocked them out right then in our meeting. For the set they needed more information on, they sent follow-up emails or set up meetings. Last, regarding the set that should never have been assigned to them, we assigned it back to the fence-tosser to find its real, rightful owner. That right there is accountability in three easy steps.

You can try it on your teams or with your own to-do lists:

• Knock off the tasks that can be done in less than three minutes.

- Do the next step to move the ball forward on the larger tasks (e.g., set up the meeting, share the proposal, ask the follow-up questions).
- Redirect the remaining tasks that shouldn't have been assigned to you in the first place to the rightful owner.

Now why hadn't Alex done these three steps on their own? Why did they let the work start to pile up before triaging all of it, especially with the amount of quick and easy tasks or things that they weren't even responsible for? When we're drowning in a sea of things that have to get done, it's difficult to see the forest for the trees. People tend to chip away at the first thing in front of them rather than the quickest thing. In addition, while it might seem obvious outside of the situation, when you're in the middle of a project and tensions are high, it's easy to just keep doing what you've been doing to keep your head above water. Rather than sit down and talk Alex through their tasks, people on the team kept piling on the work and not questioning why more and more things were overdue.

Having a conversation on expectation-setting allows all parties to get on the same page about what can actually get done and when. It narrows the ownership from something abstract and elusive to something concrete and actionable in a way that ensures we all get the results we want at the end of a project, without surprises.

OUTSMART THE DOUBLE BIND

I mentioned the double bind our collaborative and observant tendencies can put us in: We see all of the instances where accountability is missing, but then when we call for accountability, we're labeled as complainers. While that reality makes me want to flip a table, there are ways to use this to our advantage if we are intentional about it.

When we notice a situation is turning into a dumpster fire, there is a moment right before the flames start blazing where we can tap into our accountability-sensing gifts. You see, being able to sense a problem *before* it's a problem is a superpower: that's something we want to keep leaning into. What we want to reframe is *how* we communicate that there's a problem and what we do once we notice it.

Communicating a risk with a mitigation plan is not the same as complaining. And we ensure it's not seen that way by removing "I need" from the conversation. A few years ago, I was working on a project, and as the possibility of missing a deadline loomed over my head, I'd get antsy and say things like "I need you guys to finish your work," or "I need this done by 2 p.m." The irony was that the work had nothing to do with me personally; it was not something *I needed*, it was the team members' FUCKING JOB to complete it. What was I doing in this situation? Making the team accountable to me as opposed to their manager or their paycheck.

Instead of saying "I need this by 2 p.m.," try, "The proposal needs to get to the client by 2 p.m." It means *the same thing* and doesn't make someone's job seem like a personal favor to you. When I started reframing the way I spoke to my team members, they became more accountable for their work. People weren't missing deadlines because they didn't give a shit about my needs (arguable...), it was because we all knew it wasn't something *I* actually needed, so the pressure felt unwarranted. But when I connected the request to the work the team signed up to do or was responsible for, I could call for accountability and not make it about me.

Along with this strategy, when communicating a risk, I try my best to remove judgment or analysis. With an overactive Spidey sense, I've been known to jump to conclusions once or twice, maybe even suggesting there's a lack of accountability where there isn't one, if only I had all of the information. In a situation where I don't have all of the details but I see a problem starting to brew, I say something like, "Hey Manager, I'm noticing a risk that I wanted to call out, recognizing that I don't have all of the details. [Describe said risk.] Is there any more context you have on the situation you can share?" This framing is *not* to undermine my point with the "woman in a meeting" language we explored in Chapter 6 but to highlight how I actually don't have all of the information and there is a possibility that something isn't the issue I thought it was. Messaging it this way allows me to proactively share what I'm sensing without someone rolling their eyes, thinking, *Here she goes again being an alarmist.*[*]

[*] I'm not saying that interpretation is warranted, but it happens, so we might as well use some influencing strategies.

It allows the other person to consider if they're in the right headspace to discuss a problem before rolling up their sleeves. It also allows them to calibrate with me how big of a risk something is before I go spelunking for more information.

Noticing where accountability is lacking is a skill most women have locked down. Let's spread the wealth a bit. In my teams, the more I started talking about accountability framed as a question as opposed to an accusation, the more people started to think about it. The more people started thinking about it, the more I started to hear about it in meetings, and without ever having to wield a megaphone, my revolution was born. We don't need to be the only ones with overactive radars about what's going on under the surface on a team. Let's give everyone a chance to step up.

PUTTING IT TO THE TEST

Before we jump into practicing, can we all nod in agreement that the word "accountability" doesn't deserve such a bad reputation?

Reframing the general public's perception of this term will go great lengths in building a more accountable society, if that's what you're into. Just sayin'.

LET'S PRACTICE

I shared an example in this chapter about helping a team member navigate his mountainous to-do list, and it's a helpful exercise any of us can use when we're feeling overwhelmed by all that we have to get done. This exercise helps us hold ourselves accountable to doing the work on our plate and hold others accountable to the work that really belongs to them.

Block off a chunk of time, ideally an hour, but it can be done in 30 minutes if you've just had a late afternoon cold brew and are looking for a challenge.

THINK ABOUT THIS BLOCK OF TIME IN THREE DISTINCT CHUNKS:

1) Tasks that can be done in two to three minutes

2) The first/next step of the larger tasks

3) Tasks you can reassign/delegate

You now likely have a much more manageable set of tasks that consist mainly of the deeper thinking work. With the administrative and follow-up work off your plate, it should be easier to find a block of uninterrupted time to get out there and kick some work project ass.

I KNOW I'M NOT THE ONLY ONE WHO, TO THIS DAY, STILL *SOMETIMES* WISHES THEY COULD JUST TOSS A DECISION OVER TO MOM. SHE'D KNOW WHAT TO DO.

CHAPTER 12

REFRAMING DECISION-MAKING

IT WAS THREE days into starting my new role, and I knew with 100 percent certainty it wasn't a good fit. I had uprooted my life, not to mention that of my husband, who now had to hunt for a new job in a new state, and all it took was 72 hours for me to see beyond a shadow of a doubt that I'd blown it.

If I were to categorize my decision-making process in this moment (and in general), I'd say it was somewhere between endless overthinking and abrupt impulsiveness, and if that sounds confusing to you, then welcome to my brain, nice to have you, things are weird in here. When faced with a major decision (like maybe...accepting a new job in a new state) and all of the uncertainty that comes with it (finding a place to live, making friends, liking my job, hoping my husband doesn't regret *his* decision to agree to all this), I typically visualize all the directions things could go, agonize over each into the wee hours of the night, then start questioning the validity of every decision I've made in the past for an extra gut-punch, before abruptly making a decision that doesn't align with anything I agonized over (or with my long-term goals!) just to say I'm doing *something*. Exhausted? Me too.

Why do I (and, c'mon, you) do this? Why do we make this process so hard on ourselves? To start, we not only have to *make* decisions—taking a new job, pulling the plug on a project, hiring a new team member—we're expected to *live with them*, even if we immediately regret our choice. Decision-making feels final and permanent, and in a world where our inner critic second guesses everything we say and do (mine loves to recall full conversations I blundered as far back as the second grade), it's virtually impossible to feel comfortable when presented with a hard choice. Or even an easy one.

There is a wide range of reasons we struggle with decision-making, and it varies greatly depending on our upbringing. Growing up during the prelude to the era of overscheduled lives where others made most decisions for us (what friends to hang out with, what sports to play, what college to apply to), many of us became inexperienced in the act of decision-making. This isn't necessarily a bad thing—moms often make great decisions (Can you tell I'm a parent?), and most of us loved playing soccer or going to band practice or hanging out at Angela's because mom knew her parents had a pool. I know I'm not the only one who, to this day, still *sometimes* wishes they could just toss a decision over to Mom. She'd know what to do. But when we're over-reliant on help from others, we're left without the skills needed to make a decision for ourselves.

Even if that wasn't the case for you, you're not in the clear. Those perfectionist tendencies and the pressure to be everything for everyone can make us indecisive; we're caught wondering whether each specific decision will be the one that causes us to fall short of the expectations others have of us. I spend most of my time carrying the weight of not wanting to disappoint others, which means every time I make even a minor decision it feels like I'm working for the United Nations. And when it comes to making the tougher calls, I am dragged down by perfectionism and rumination's love child, "analysis paralysis," and get completely stuck. *What if I make the wrong move? What if people think I'm stupid? What if I ruin my life?* See ALL chapters leading up to this one for tips on how to deal with those questions.

Does the spiral go deeper? Yup. Guilt. If we're afraid to disappoint or we think we disappointed others, it becomes another weight pulling us down. *Why did I choose that? Why did I make that move? Why am I such an idiot?* Our fixed mindset compelling us to get everything right creates those pangs of gut-punching regret when we feel like we got something wrong, and we end up buried in the anxiety of uncertainty and shame. As women, we know opportunities are scarce, and we don't know when the next one will present itself, if ever. The pressure to nail it the first time maps straight to being people-pleasing perfectionists whose egos want other people to think we made the right call.

Or maybe, we've burst through these barriers and embrace making decisions, only to be stopped in our tracks and told what we're doing is wrong. "You're gonna wear *that*?" "I know you interviewed 15 people for the role and think Suze is the best for the project, but maybe we should just check with Tyler to see what he thinks."* In many environments, our decisions are second-guessed or we have to bring in more data and evidence to explain our thought process...only to be told we need to get to the point.

*Good thing Tyler was there to speak on our behalf or we might have been forced to make an actual decision on our own. Thanks for squeezing us in, Ty!

Sooooo, yeah, it's a clusterfuck. I've been stuck in each of these traps, often at the same time. But when I look back at some of the decisions I felt were huge mistakes or that took me in a radically different direction than I had initially anticipated, after the dust settled, they were never actually *that bad*. The majority of decisions we make on any given day impact at most a few months or years into the future, but rarely forever. Which means they don't always end in disaster and disappointment. When I moved for that job, the time I spent on the team resulted in an incredible amount of personal and professional growth, even though I never really felt at home in the new role. My husband ended up landing a job he loved. We settled down closer to family and made some fantastic new friendships. To say this decision was an epic fail wouldn't be anywhere near accurate.

Believe me, I roll my eyes at the cliché that "success is not a straight line" just as much as the next person, but, my friends, it *isn't*. We all want the process to be easier, but the best kind of growth comes out of decisions that are hard. And it was only when I started reframing my relationship with the finality of decisions that I felt ready and safe to give more things a try.

KNOW THYSELF

But how do I know what to decide?!

Ah, the million-dollar question.

Knowing what path to take in an uncertain situation requires connecting back to what we *are* certain about. We talked about values in Chapter 4 as we dove into exploring goal setting. When facing a career- or life-altering decision, we can start by using the very same tools: connecting to the core of what matters most to us, what has to be true no matter what decision we're faced with making.

Our values can point to the environments we want to be in (integrity, accountability, achievement), the types of structure we want to have (freedom, flexibility, order) and the kinds of people we want to be surrounded by (inclusion, belonging, empathy, power). The sum of each of these signals gives us insight into what has to be true in a job in order to have a long-term future there.

In *The Confidence Gap,* the book we explored in Chapter 6 as we delved into the fears that stifle confidence, Russ Harris writes that "your values describe how you want to behave as a human being: how you want to act on an ongoing basis, what you want to stand for in life, the principles you want to live by, the personal qualities and character strengths you want to cultivate." When we anchor to our values, even if an individual decision doesn't set us on the course we thought it would, we know it was made in service of honoring what's important to us. We're resilient when we encounter setbacks (as opposed to berating ourselves with "why" questions) because we're focused on the bigger picture.

Our values also serve as guardrails to help us weigh decisions. We can ask ourselves, "Does this career change from middle manager to senior director line up with my value of flexibility, or will it get in the way of that?"* With societal pressures like achievement and financial success, understanding our personal values helps us prioritize what's important to us.

When my coaching clients or mentees come to me wanting more certainty about a tough decision they are navigating, I ask them to start by imagining a picture, at some

*We all know "flexibility" is code for "take Fridays off and kickstart my weekly attempt to take up intermittent fasting."

point in the future, where they are doing the things they want in their careers. Are they teaching and mentoring, are they leading, are they unlocking new discoveries? Each of these signals gives them a sense of what is important for them in a role in order for it to be fulfilling. With these goal posts set, we can then map the path toward getting them there.

For example, when I realized I had made a career change that wasn't right for me, I tried to tune into what was missing to better understand why the role wasn't a fit. My value of connection fuels my need to work more closely on organizational dynamics, and the reason I wasn't feeling the job was because it didn't allow me to do that. I didn't know exactly what that would entail, but I knew in order for me to feel fulfilled, my work would have to center on people-related responsibilities. With this baseline, I could look at what I was doing at that moment, examine what aspects of the current role would help support this future endeavor and consider what roles would be the next practical step to getting me closer to my ideal job.

It may still take time to come to a decision, but in understanding how these signals map to our values, we can make them with confidence. Instead of that dreaded punch-in-the-stomach feeling of panic when someone asks "Why did you choose *that*?" we can calmly explain how our choice connects to the bigger story of what's important to us. And then tell them to mind their fucking business.

IT'S ALL AN EXPERIMENT

When we're clear on our values, decisions can be fluid. But if you're anything like me, thinking *WTF is "fluid" supposed to mean when I'm talking about my career or salary?!*, don't worry, I've got some tools to share.

I mentioned that for me the heart of reframing decision-making comes from forming a new relationship with the finality of decisions, made possible by treating my decisions as "experiments." In tech, "experiment" is a fancy word for "no one knows what the hell will happen, so let's just give it a try," which, if we're being honest with ourselves, is really the state wherein we make most decisions, right?

Experimentation implies there's a shorter time frame, that you are going to try something, evaluate if it's working and fine tune it along the way. It allows for flexibility and fluidity, because adjusting different variables is part of what makes something an experiment in the first place.

To demonstrate an experimentation framework, I toyed with just sharing the legit seventh grade science class Scientific Method since it's a pretty tried and true model, but I decided to create something special just for you. For the sake of science, mine also has five steps. We'll call this framework "Thrive in Five" and use the example of deciding to pursue a degree or certification in addition to having a day job.

Step 1: Get crystal clear on the decision you need to make, including any sub-decisions that come with it.
Ex: Deciding which program gives me the best training with the most flexibility, where to cut spending to save for the cost, when to make time for classes and studying during the week.

Step 2: Consider the ultimate goal of your decision and which of your values the decision honors.
Ex: Supports my value of continual learning and my goal to take on more of a leadership position on my team.

Step 3: Determine the intervals for checking in.

Ex: Every few weeks to make sure I'm not underwater balancing work and studying.

Step 4: Check in to see if the decision is leading you to your goal.

Ex: My fancy new skills allowed me to take on more strategic work and I was asked to lead a project! Win!

Step 5: Identify anything you need to fine tune about your decision or sub-decisions to stay on course.

Ex: But...I'm working more than I want to be, so I need to continue to set boundaries and practice more delegation.

Using a framework like this reminds us we'll have opportunities to check in and revisit if things don't feel quite right. It helps us dodge the useless question of "Where do you see yourself in five years?" as if a decision we make today in *this* job really has that much control over the next 1,825 days. In 2020, the world turned upside down, and major industries like hospitality, travel, event planning and late-night bar-hopping came to a grinding halt. By the time you're reading this, some billionaire might have walked on Mars. *No one* knows what the hell they are going to be doing in five years. Most of us just imagine our current roles and think *not doing this* but that's all we can come up with. Let it be vague, let it be open-ended.

Instead of focusing on *getting* it right (remember: we debunked "right" like five chapters ago), focus on it *feeling* right. Experimenting allows us to take inventory of our decisions with curiosity as opposed to judgment and doubt, giving us the resilience to withstand a bumpy road because we know what we're driving toward. When I chose to relocate for a job, there was more than just liking the job that made the move worth it, and that helped fight some of the shame I had over feeling like I made a bad call. But in the end, periodically evaluating my progress along the way shined light on the fact that the job had an expiration date, and that was OK. And it helped propel me toward deciding my next move, which turned out marginally better. Baby steps.

TRUST YOUR GUT

Flash forward a few years, and I've made another change in jobs and feel that same sinking feeling in the pit of my stomach that signals the situation isn't right for me.

First question to myself: *Are you fucking kidding me?!*

Second question: *No, really, are you fucking KIDDING ME?!?!*

OK, third question: *What did I learn from my earlier experience that I can apply here?*

Having lived through it once before, I already knew that no job is forever, that this didn't have to be the place I'd work 'til the social security checks kicked in. I knew that when I feel this way, I should trust my gut and start making my game plan for finding the next opportunity.

Now, I mean it when I suggest we trust our gut. Countless women have shared stories with me about rough situations at work where they are undervalued and underappreciated, not getting the opportunities they deserve based on the effort they are putting in—they're stuck deciding what to do next. I've spoken about how the world isn't fair, but that's not an invitation to stay in a bad situation you know isn't right for you.

If we continually doubt our decision-making skills or haven't had many opportunities to make decisions for ourselves, it can be easy to stop listening to our feelings and instincts. But when we do this, we also lose the important skill of discerning between our pessimistic inner critic that thinks everything is terrible and our optimistic sense of self that wants the best for us. These are two very different things, and trusting our gut is about knowing, with appreciation, clarity and ease, that it's time to make a move. And if you have to stay in the situation for the time being, trusting your gut is about tuning into what boundaries you need to set to make it more tolerable.

When the helpful self (aka the gut) is talking, it recognizes we're not being utilized to the best of our abilities. It considers a variety of ways to approach a problem and demonstrate our value, and if they're not embraced, recognizes the hard truth that we can't change other people. The helpful self is excited to seek out new opportunities knowing it learns from each experience, and that even the most challenging situations don't last forever.

In round two of taking a job I realized wasn't a match, I learned the hard lesson that just because you're right for a team doesn't mean the team is right for you. I was offered a great opportunity, the team was awesome and I figured I'd learn to like the work. Only I didn't. Once I was able to swat away the inner critic, I tuned into my gut and asked myself: *What pattern is present that I'm ignoring?*

I recently shared this tip with a colleague navigating the decision to become a people manager. Everyone had been telling her it was a great opportunity for her career and to go for it, but her gut said otherwise. She was a very ambitious person and was great at recognizing the right next step in her career, but she was stuck wondering who was skeptical of the opportunity, her gut or her inner critic. I asked her to share what her gut told her, and she spoke about how she had plenty of opportunities to mentor and help develop others; she just didn't want to pile performance management on top of her existing workload. Then I asked, "If that's the case, what's getting in the way of making the decision?"

"Everyone *else's* expectations." Bingo.

Our two questions: "What pattern is present that I'm ignoring?" and "What's getting in the way of making the decision?" generally lead us to the same conclusion: We're so lost navigating the sea of what everyone else wants that we forget about what *we* want.

Trusting our gut means, well, *trusting* ourselves to make the right decision, given everything we know about the situation. It's about making the choice that feels more authentic to our values and goals, as opposed to getting lured in by the expectations of others.

This can feel scary in that it might fuel the inner critic telling us we're passing up a great opportunity. But what's so great about an opportunity if we're not invested in it, decide to pursue it for the wrong reasons or can't be ourselves once we get there? As we sharpen our reframing skills—believing we are capable of achieving our goals, setting boundaries and asking for what we need—confidence in making decisions is at the center. We are the ones who, at the end of the day, must live with our decisions, even if a colleague or manager made a *highly* compelling argument for making it. Trusting our gut means believing we know what's best for ourselves, and as we get closer to that feeling, it can be incredibly useful to enlist the help of a framework.

IT'S A PROCESS

After reflecting on my decision-making fails, and when writing this chapter I was faced with thinking about what my ideal process would be. As always, it was easier to start by exploring what I *wouldn't* do.

While researching decision-making, you generally come across the suggestion to make a pros and cons list, as if every single item carries equal weight. If you have three pros and two cons, the clear answer is to go for it, even if one of the cons is that you'd rather get mauled by a bear than move forward with the decision. Pros and cons can help you get raw ideas onto paper, but the process grossly overestimates how much insight you have into what the future will look like and frames the scenario as an unchanging picture. For example, if you're weighing taking on additional responsibilities at work, the pro of adding more value doesn't last forever, nor does the con of the work taking up more of your time. Both of those factors can change in a matter of months, while you're still poring over your list wondering where you went wrong.

For a process on what *to* do, I'll borrow from the best. Chip and Dan Heath study patterns in behavior and action across a series of bestselling books they've partnered on. In *Decisive*, they explore how to overcome our biases and tendencies to jump to snap decisions, offering a four-step framework for decision-making. Their process, WRAP, suggests you "Widen Your Options," "Reality-Test Your Assumptions," "Attain Distance Before Deciding" and "Prepare to Be Wrong."

Examining each step in the process through the lens of the traps and tools we've discussed throughout this book reveals this framework's incredible utility. When we widen our options, we see that there is rarely only one path forward, one way something could go well, one conclusion to be drawn. From there, reality testing our assumptions allows us to bring in the "What's the worst that could happen?" tool we explored in Chapter 6, reminding ourselves that when a decision isn't going the way we want, we can course correct. Attaining distance before making the decision prevents us from allowing our inner critic to quickly make the call for us, letting the expansive thinking process of the first two steps settle in. Last, preparing to be wrong is about not getting trapped in "what if" land. If we *could* predict the future, we would have bought a lottery ticket or played the stock market right YEARS ago and would no longer be caught up in any of this work shit. But since we can't, this step is about proactively planting seeds for what's next for you, so when something inevitably ends up different than we expected, we have a productive way out or frame for how to look at it.

Making decisions thoughtfully can take time...but too much time can start to work against us. A looming uncertainty over the right decision can breed inertia, and I've found that too much inertia over a long period of time creates a pressure cooker when it comes to making decisions. We keep adding things to the pot and cranking up the heat, waiting, waiting, waiting, and when the lid finally pops, we dive for cover toward a direction we hadn't intended.

I'll say it again—reframing the finality of our decisions is powerful, and this framework helps reinforce that. When we prepare to be wrong, we release ourselves from the hold of the fixed mindset that tells us decisions have to be perfect or that we're inherently *bad* at decision-making. Instead, we understand decisions are fluid, and even if we make a decision that suggests we were momentarily overtaken by the decision-making short-sightedness of a fourth grader, it means the *decision* was bad, not that *we* are bad.

We have no way of knowing exactly what will happen from day to day, year to year. Holding on too tightly to having it all figured out can leave us feeling stuck. And we're stuck in an illusion, because again, we can never really know. As I reflect on my own decisions and coach others through their own feelings of uncertainty, I'm reminded not to look at situations as binary or permanent. Everything is on a continuum.

So what if you're wrong? So what if you don't like it? Trust yourself to find a path forward in situations when something didn't end up being the way you hoped it to be. If we never try, we never know. And take it from me, NOTHING leads to more rumination than wondering what might have been.

PUTTING IT TO THE TEST

We will encounter hard decisions throughout our entire lives. The key is not to avoid them but to lean into these tools to make them feel less permanent and more manageable. Remember, *not* making a decision *is* a decision.

LET'S PRACTICE

Using our "Thrive in Five" experimentation framework, consider a decision that has been weighing on you or is something that's likely coming up in the near future, and answer the following questions:

Step 1) Clarifying the decision: What are the additional baby decisions that might come along with the big decision?

Step 2) Identifying the goal: What does this decision enable for you, and what values does it connect to?

Step 3) Timing: When does it make sense to check in on progress?

Step 4) Checking in: What does incremental success look like?

Step 5) Fine-tuning: What can you tweak to get back on course, or has a newer, *better* course presented itself that you want to follow?

Answering these questions helps take some of the pressure off having to get everything right on the first try, demonstrating that there's generally space to evolve and fine-tune.

YES,
WE COMPARE.
WE COMPETE.
AND
WE BRING
THE HEAT.

CHAPTER 13

REFRAMING COMPARISON

TO SAY I struggle with comparison is the understatement of the decade, a decade that began with me stating 2020 would be the year I'd try to spend a little more time at home.

On good days, I'll dip into a little dose of Instagram to wallow in my lack of traveling enough before snapping out of it and re-membering how much I hate airports. On bad days, however, the rabbit hole goes deep. What starts as admiring the latest vaca-tion pics from Tan France's adventures quickly escalates to being down on myself for not having advanced as fast in my career as the people I went to high school with and looking around my house wondering why it's such a mess when my friends with more kids and pets can manage to keep their homes clean and their lives #blessed. We all know what we see online is completely curated, and yet we still get those pangs of self-criticism when we're scrolling and see the accomplishments or travels or suc-cesses of our friends, people we barely remember or celebrities we've never met.*

Even if you aren't on social media, you're not free of the death grip of self-deprecating comparison. It happens at work ALL OF THE TIME. We look at the people around us and start to assess how we measure up. We watch our peers get promoted and question if we're working hard enough. If a person we view as successful is older, we wonder, *Will I be at that level when I'm their age?* If they're younger, *Why has it taken me so long to rise up the ranks?* If they're another woman, *What does she have that I don't?* And if they're a man, we think, *This is pointless. I'll never have what he has.*

Stopping this cycle of comparison isn't easy. In fact, it might be the hardest thing I've asked you to do in this entire book. Many people get stuck trying to "keep up with the Joneses," but often, women take this to a whole other level. Television, magazines, movies, our workplace, society at large—everything everywhere is constantly telling women we have to be nice, thin, beautiful, smart, well liked, helpful, accommodating, calm and more and more and fucking more. We have to aspire toward a standard that is both utterly manufactured and completely unattainable. When we look around and see others who seem like they've got it all figured out (which no one actually does), we start to judge. *Why can't I be more like her? Why am I so stressed but she has it so easy?* We also start to resent. *She's not even that pretty—why is she getting all that attention? She's not even that smart—how did she get that promotion?*

Comparison is consuming. When we don't get a hold of

it, it surfaces at the wrong moments and can cause others to recoil. We think dropping a little hint about how someone isn't doing something the way they should or doesn't deserve what they have goes unnoticed, but it doesn't. This behavior attracts other comparers and repels people who don't want to fall into the trap. Soon you become surrounded only by those in the same painful cycle of comparison and resentment, and it's even harder to break free. *

BREAK THE CYCLE

Comparison is the ultimate expression of the question "Am I enough?"—which is why it's so seductive.

*All of whom are hanging out with you because they think they're at least marginally better than you.

When we compare ourselves to someone and feel worse, we reinforce the inner critic's narrative that we're lacking in some way. When we compare ourselves and feel better, we're riding on the endorphin hit of temporarily believing we are superior to someone. But even if we momentarily feel better, comparing ourselves to others still doesn't make us feel like we're enough, because the never-ending cycle kicks off again the moment someone else has something we want.

In *The Gifts of Imperfection*, Brené Brown's book that I discussed in Chapter 11 while exploring accountability, Brené suggests, "Given how difficult it is to cultivate self-acceptance in our perfectionist society and how our need for belonging is hardwired, it's no wonder that we spend our lives trying to fit in and gain approval." Yep. That.

To try to fit in, we start comparing. And as we're comparing, we start judging, and—you guessed it—the beast keeps feeding itself.

The Confidence Gap by Russ Harris, which we explored in Chapters 6 and 12, discusses strategies for releasing the hold negative thoughts and fears have over us so we can take the meaningful actions that result in a greater sense of confidence. *Sign me up!* Russ uses the analogy of being hooked like a fish on a line with no escape when we're "hooked" by a negative thought and start getting reeled into believing it's true. We can use the power of self-awareness we've honed throughout the course of this book to pause, reframe and remind ourselves that our thoughts do not dictate our actions. Fortunately for humans, not so fortunately for fish, we have the power to "unhook"...or get unstuck. Wink face. Russ calls this action "defusion," as in de-fusing from our limiting beliefs. By creating a mental separation between who we are and what our thoughts are saying, we give ourselves room to release the hold our judgmental or comparative thoughts have over us.

Defusion allows us to recognize when judgment and comparison are present *without judging those thoughts.* Often when I'm in a new situation, I'm a *bit* of a skeptic. Whether it's a class, event, training session or something I signed up for in advance and paid money for, I'm guilty of immediately sizing it up and judging whether or not it's a good use of my time.* As you can imagine, this cycle pulls me out of the present and makes it hard to get over the skeptical bias and actually find enjoyment or value in it.

Knowing this about myself, I started to deploy the tactic of defusion. When I catch myself hooked in a judgmental

*And being the patient person I am, I'm always hoping the thing, whatever it is, will end early.

or skeptical thought pattern, I pause and reflect. *Ah, this negative thought is me being nervous since I took on extra work lately, putting more pressure on the situation to be mind-blowing and worth my precious free time.* When I recognize what is driving the thought, I can reframe. *Since I'm already here, what do I need to get the most out of this experience?* Sometimes I don't find it. Which is why I never make plans on Monday nights.

CATCH AND RELEASE

If you're having trouble recognizing when you are comparing, a good place to start is by examining the thoughts that make you feel sad, frustrated or not good enough—there's nearly always some element of comparison associated with those emotions. When you figure out where you've had the tendency to compare in the past, you can start to notice when it's happening in real time.

Along with checking in with your thought processes, remember to reflect on the questions you ask yourself. We discussed the importance of shifting from "why" to "what" in our ego chapter, and this is a critical step when it comes to comparative thoughts. *Why did they get that thing and not me?* doesn't give ourselves anything to work with. There isn't an answer to that question that doesn't heap on the judgment; that question is looking to stir shit up. Instead, try asking yourself, *What is it that's making me want this thing?* Yikes, OK, now I have no choice *but* to reflect.

My strategy for breaking the judgment/comparison cycle once I've noticed it? I ask myself two questions:

- Do I really want *this*?
- If not, what is it I *actually* want?

Sometimes we think we want one thing because we are lacking in another area. For example, we might think we want to travel more, when what we actually want is change. Other times, yeah, New Zealand. Looks amazing. I don't need to search my soul to know I want to hang out in Middle-earth. We distinguish between these two types of desires by reminding ourselves what actually matters to us (i.e., our values and purpose) and not getting sidetracked by the allure of what our comparison tendencies tell us we should want.

When our default response to seeing literally *anything* out in the world is to judge or compare, we're falsely falling into a trap of thinking we want that thing. But if we're able to ask ourselves *What is it I actually want?* when we catch ourselves comparing, we can differentiate between the experiences we want and the things those experiences might represent.

I once had a colleague, Ben, who had an Airstream camper van, and he'd often show pictures of his glorious camping adventures on Mondays at work. I'm not a camper myself, but the sleek design of an Airstream and potential to hit the open road at a moment's notice started to become appealing enough to judge myself for not having one. Oh...and also for not being spontaneous enough.* But, wait a second—I *literally* just said I didn't like camping. So what the fuck was it that I actually wanted? I wanted something in my life to nudge me to explore more or be more adventurous, but I didn't need an Airstream to make that happen. That was Ben's dream, not mine. As I reflected on this desire to be more spontaneous, I could start to make plans that were more authentic to me, like springing for a fun dinner on a

*You mean "lying on my couch sipping Black Cherry White Claw while swiping TikTok" isn't exciting?

weeknight (not a Monday, of course!) or taking a day trip to a new place. When I did these things, I felt genuine enjoyment, with the bonus of not having to worry about whether the experience would live up to expectations that weren't even mine in the first place.

EMBRACE THE FOMO

Executive coaching was something I had been wanting to get into for a while; I just hadn't made it a priority to get started. Then I received an email from a colleague who was pursuing coaching and looking for clients to work with for hours toward her certification. When I saw this, I immediately thought, *Hey!! Why am I not doing that?* Then I started a comparing/judging cycle, berating myself for not having gotten started with coaching, telling myself *I don't have any time to do what I want now that I have a baby, it's too late for me to learn a new thing,* and comparing, comparing, comparing.

Fortunately, after only a few minutes I caught myself, paused the unproductive pity spiral and reframed.* *Wow...I didn't even realize how important this coaching thing was to me before I got that email. Now it's all I can think about.* I decided to let myself out of the judgment loop and instead used it as a launchpad to start exploring coaching programs.

At times, FOMO can be helpful. It can signal a goal that was dormant, waiting to be unearthed. In these moments, we might have needed the kick in the pants from someone else doing something we were also interested in doing to show us that it's actually more attainable than we thought. Through observing your reactions objectively (read: with-

*We all know it was way more than a few minutes.

out judgment), this comparison might clarify something we didn't realize we actually wanted. Again, the key is to observe our thoughts from a place of non-judgment so we have control over deciding how to respond instead of falling into the default *I'm not enough* thought pattern. Spoiler: *I'm a loser and can't even recognize my own goals* is still pretty judgy.

The difference between embracing FOMO and being consumed by it lies in what you do once the feeling comes over you. By leveraging the tools in Chapter 4 and getting crystal clear on our goals, we can first validate that this "thing" we want really ladders up to something that's important to us. Then, we leverage the tools we discussed in Chapter 12 about decision-making and launch an experiment.

In my coaching example, my FOMO immediately pushed me into action, researching options and signing up for a course. Knowing myself, I could have easily spent the next six or so months (conservative estimate) weighing all of the possibilities, further getting behind on this goal I had, even after it was clear I wanted it. Fortunately, in a moment of clarity, I was able to embrace my FOMO and go for it.

If you're stuck in the trap of analysis paralysis once you've decided you want something, what are you waiting for? Let's use FOMO with surgical precision, recognizing the moment when it's the last signal we need to take the plunge. This means religiously deploying those two questions we discussed (Do I want *this*? and If not, what is it I *actually* want?), and when the answer to the first is YES, start taking action. The best part is, once we get moving into action, our feelings of FOMO begin to dissipate because we're *not* missing out.

CRACK THE CHAMPAGNE

I've spent the entirety of this book talking about the double standards and biases that make it so hard to feel confident in our work, in who we are and in what we bring to the table. Sometimes, the measuring stick created by comparison is the necessary jolt to get us to take action. But when it leads to resenting the accomplishments of other women, it has far exceeded any helpfulness and only makes us feel worse.

Competition is yet another pitfall of the comparison pattern, often fueled by the limited number of opportunities afforded to women. This can even go as far as *I don't want that thing, but I sure as hell don't want Nicole to have it.* Safe space, you don't have to admit it, but I'm guessing we've all been there at least once.

Remember my friend Sarah from Chapter 5, the one who got promoted to be her friend's manager? I told my friend Owen about that situation and his response was eye-opening: "I would love to be managed by a friend," he said. "They would know me and my work style. I'd be happy for them for getting a promotion. It would be great."

I'm sorry...come again? I had no idea what to say. I know I'm making a whopping generalization here, but I don't know a single woman who would have that reaction. Even when we are close with our team members, because there are so few positions for women at the top of the corporate ladder (or as heads of state, or as NFL coaches or in whatever arena in which men have filled the majority of the high-ranking positions), no matter who you are going up against, when you're a woman, it always feels like you are in competition. In a society that is still patting itself on the back for having *one woman* in a C-suite, there are legitimately a limited number of spots being filled by women. So yes, we compare. We compete. And we bring the heat.

My tool for breaking the competitive resentment cycle when another woman achieves something? Celebrating it.[*]

*And genuinely celebrating it, not sending a "Congratulations" text with a party popper emoji as you roll your eyes to your friends over how the person doesn't deserve it.

The beauty of celebrating is that we can do it as often as we want. We don't have a finite number of "great job" tickets we can hand out until we've exhausted them. And the more we celebrate others, the wider our community becomes, and the more people we have in our network to celebrate us when it's our turn.

When we toast to the successes of other women, we remind ourselves that achieving great things is possible. With the exception of someone getting selected for the exact job or promotion you were going for, most of the successes of others aren't things we were in direct competition for. And don't we want people who are rising through the ranks to be in our corner as we're reaching toward our next goals?

Thinking back to my conversation with Owen, I realized how backward we get it sometimes. What purpose does it serve us to resent that person or decide in advance that a situation is going to be terrible before it's set into motion? It only makes us feel worse, more frustrated with ourselves, more dissatisfied with our progress toward our own goals.

Instead of thinking *I could have done that*, try reframing to *I can do that*. Let's use our instinct to compare to propel us toward the goals and aspirations we have for ourselves. Let's use it to light a path toward realizing our goals. Let's ask people further ahead on their journey for guidance, insights, help, even. We might just find there's value we can share back to the person we thought had it all figured out. But that's only possible if we haven't already decided we have no use for that person.

In *The Gifts of Imperfection*, Brené reminds us that so much of the feelings of shame we have when we feel we are not enough stem from feeling isolated. When we celebrate others, we remind ourselves we're not alone. The more we connect to others, the more support we have to overcome the challenges we've talked about throughout this book, and the more we can help others overcome them.

When I reframed any feelings of resentment to celebrate the successes of my colleagues, I realized how inspiring they were to me, as well as how attainable my own goals actually were. And I knew I could get there because I had the support and encouragement of the community I had supported and encouraged. That cycle was a lot more fun and a hell of a lot more productive.

Flipping the switch from judgment to celebration isn't easy, but one way to get there is through mindfulness. Mindfulness is the practice of being aware of the present moment, and when it comes to comparing ourselves to others, we're literally doing everything BUT being present. Being aware of our thought patterns is the act of mindfulness, and the faster we catch ourselves analyzing the moment instead of living in it, the faster we're able to really experience it.

At the center of being present is gratitude. Given that our comparative thoughts come from a place of not feeling like we're enough, appreciating who we are and what we have is an effective strategy for quieting the negative thoughts. I know it's not instant, especially if we've had a shitty day, but if we can end each day thinking about three things we appreciate or are grateful for, we will go to bed happier and wake up more refreshed. Don't take it from me, take it from the whole booming industry of gratitude journals.

Shifting to expressing gratitude can feel like an uphill battle when all the odds are against us, but it's easier to push against the obstacles when we recognize and appreciate the things we do have on our side. Try practicing gratitude with small things at first, like someone smiling at you on the bus, the eloquent email you sent, the absence of traffic on your way home from work. All of these things together, over time, start to create a reality of abundance rather than scarcity.

In *Enough As She Is*, Rachel Simmons reminds us that we start to feel like we're enough when we're able to replace comparison and the expectations everyone *else* has with our *own* vision of fulfillment and purpose. We will always feel like we're on a never-ending hamster wheel if we don't stop and reflect on what we want, what's important to us and what we care about. We can stop this cycle by changing our perspective. When we reframe our tendency to compare into a tendency to appreciate and celebrate, we recognize we already have so much of what we want, and the goals that seemed so far out of reach are truly right there for the taking.

PUTTING IT TO THE TEST

We're programmed to continually size ourselves up to see if we're good enough. But the more we compare, the worse we feel, and the more vicious the cycle.

In the ultimate reframe of all, let's think about what nugget of value we can find from comparative thoughts.

LET'S PRACTICE

Think about three things in your life that have been kicking your FOMO into high gear. *Everyone is getting married, everyone is having babies, everyone is more successful than me* kinds of thoughts.

Pick the ONE thing that you actually care about that is most aligned with your values and the aspirations you have for yourself.

- What about that one thing is important to you?
- What is the first step you can take toward making it a reality?
- When can you start? *Oh, now?* Then let's do this!

WHEN SOMEONE TELLS ME TO "LOOK ON THE BRIGHT SIDE," I WANT TO PUNCH THEM IN THE FACE.

CHAPTER 14

THAT'S NOT REFRAMING

I ONCE HAD a colleague who rarely followed through with what she said she was going to do and was always quick to point out why *not doing it* was actually better. As if that weren't bad enough, if she missed a deadline and someone else had to pick up the slack, she'd insist that person was more suited to do the job anyway. To be honest...I've had many colleagues like this.

As a person suffering from an acute case of overachiever syndrome and with an inner critic so noisy it's virtually impossible for me to think of excuses on my feet, this drove me nuts.* I shared my frustration with a mutual friend, who knew I was writing this book. "Not to be devil's advocate," she said, "but technically wouldn't you call what she's doing reframing?" Touché. I was stumped for a minute. "I guess so?" I semi-responded, wishing I hadn't given in so easily, but I didn't have a rebuttal ready. Probably be-

*Thought I was cured of judging? It's a work in progress.

cause nine times out of 10, anything that comes after "not to be devil's advocate" is worthy of an exaggerated eye roll.

But "I guess so" is not "yes," and as I thought more about it, it dawned on me why this type of behavior isn't reframing, especially in the terms I've laid out in this book. Making excuses. Alternative facts. Looking on the bright side. Exploiting the silver lining. None of these, my friends, are what I mean when I talk about "reframing." And now that you're an expert in reframing, you can help me set the record straight.

Reframing requires noticing when your perspective isn't serving you in a situation, and that can be really scary. Old habits die hard. Maybe we want to make a change in our lives but we don't have the confidence, or we're afraid to fail, or we don't trust ourselves to make the right calls. It can be easy to start to squirm away from a reframe and think, *Maybe this shitty job I dread getting out of bed in the morning to do for shitty pay isn't so bad after all...*

To seal the deal on what reframing is and isn't, we're going to spend this chapter doing some serious Myth Busting.*

* Without that ridiculous beret.

MYTH 1: REFRAMING IS LOOKING ON THE BRIGHT SIDE

Ah, the bright side. When I'm feeling really stuck, frustrated or upset and someone tells me to "look on the bright side," I want to punch them in the face. Like, what the fuck do they know about my situation that they feel justified to oversimplify it in that way? What bright side exists when I've just realized I'm getting paid too little because I didn't negotiate? Or worse, when I've just realized I'm getting paid less than my male counterpart with the same experience doing the same job?

I think it's all in the delivery here, because in any situation I do believe there is something to learn. And sure, that's a positive. But when reframing is positioned as a bright side, it invalidates and diminishes the complexity of a situation. As opposed to unshakable bright side-y optimism causing us to get wrapped up in false expectations, ignore our gut feelings or stay in bad situations too long, reframing is about knowing that there is always more than one way to look at any situation.

Our reframe for this myth is asking ourselves "What can I learn from this?" In each of the mistakes I've made throughout my career (which, as you've read, there have been plenty of), I always asked myself this question way later than I wish I had.

With my negotiation fails, I learned that in avoiding negotiating due to fears of getting it wrong, not being informed or not wanting to ask for too much, I was letting someone else set the terms of my value. By considering this question earlier, I could have earned more money sooner, saved myself countless hours of rumination and avoided numerous awkward conversations with the checkout clerk at Safeway who presumed I was having a party because of all of the Ben & Jerry's I was buying.* And when I finally did get it right, being clear on what I learned would have helped me replicate it for the next time.

*Yes, I am. Pity party of one.

When we learn things about ourselves and our needs, we

become better versions of ourselves. We are more able to practice gratitude and appreciate the things we have or got right. With this knowledge and acceptance, our growth mindset is better equipped to guide our path. All of these are "bright" possibilities, yes, but they don't ignore the struggle we went through to get there. So the next time someone asks you to look on the bright side, beyond learning that this person is likely very uncomfortable with discomfort, reframe to asking what you can learn about what you want to do, not do, say, ask or try for the next time.

MYTH 2: REFRAMING JUST GETS ME TO THE SAME SHITTY PERSPECTIVE

This brings us to our second myth: thinking we've landed on a new perspective when we're really still trapped in the same one. In the same way false optimism doesn't serve us, getting stuck in a limiting perspective where our inner critic is at the wheel also holds us back from seeing what's possible.

Whether a limiting perspective has been imparted on us by society (ex: women can't do math…even though it was fucking WOMEN who sent the first astronauts to the moon) or by ourselves (ex: *I made a bad decision, therefore I am bad at making decisions*), we inevitably start to internalize it as a universal truth, causing us to look for data that reinforces that perspective.

Take, for example, weighing a decision about changing jobs when you don't have confidence in your decision-making skills. You might think that staying in your current role is one option and taking the new role is the other, but if you're not trusting yourself to make the right call, you're only looking through *one* frame: that you make bad decisions and will get it wrong. With this perspective, neither option can be right.

When we think we've weighed all potential options and are still stuck, we're likely weighing eerily similar versions of the same limited, shitty options. No wonder the outcomes are unappealing!

Want to know the biggest secret to reframing, the one I've waited all the way till the last chapter to reveal?

Are you sitting down...?

The third option.

When you find yourself running up against a wall, even though you *think* you've looked at your options through different frames, try a curveball perspective. So many times we look at the choices we have ahead of ourselves as binary alternatives with the same weight—*stay or go, buy or sell, fight or flight, sink or swim.* What if instead we tried to *work part-time while launching a side hustle? Live in an Airbnb for a month in three new cities before deciding where to move? Share difficult feedback with a friend before telling them it's over and ghosting their texts?* All of those sound like much more interesting opportunities, none of which were limited by the false choice of picking one thing or the other. The third option is about thinking bigger and bolder.

When we feel stuck, even incremental progress can feel like a huge change, making it hard to imagine what else is out there. Brainstorming wild perspectives—even things we might never do or wouldn't even be interested in—breaks the seal on our sense of what's possible, raising the ceiling on what we might want to try. We often learn that many of our wild ideas aren't so out there after all.

The third option is where creativity exists, where dreams are made, where goals are realized. It's where you do the real work toward getting what you want.

MYTH 3: REFRAMING
MEANS MAKING EXCUSES

As a planner-advancer (a word I made up to mean the opposite of a procrastinator), when I'm asked to do something I don't want to do, I start to panic. Finishing my checklist is a stress reliever for me, so I always aim to get started right away on something I dread doing so it's not hanging over my head. One of my biggest triggers, the one that drives me toward excuses, is event planning. Too many details, too many variables, too much risk that you put all of this work in and no one comes or likes it or has fun, spiral spiral spiral. When I'm asked to plan an event, I start getting *real* creative, like "manufacturing relatives with elaborate complicated needs that I am responsible for" creative.*

The reason for this isn't that I'm full of shit or lazy or irresponsible—it's because I'm afraid to set boundaries or advocate for myself. Reframing isn't about making excuses, and it's not about just sucking it up and doing it either—it's about understanding what's getting in your way.

A few years ago I was managing an engineer, and one afternoon, I was gleefully going about my day when I glanced down at my phone and saw he had resigned via email and assigned all of his work to me. I stood up, walked into the hallway and almost threw up right there on the carpet.*

Instead of thinking, *OK, looks like I'll have to find someone to cover this work,* I thought to myself, *Oh my god, I'm going to have work nights and weekends learning how to be a fucking engineer so I can get all of this done.*

*"I would love to plan this networking event, but my Aunt Freda needs to get her scuba certification by the end of this week in order to join her volunteer trip to save the Arctic whales, and I promised I'd help her with her paperwork."

*Hard to keep a poker face in a meeting and pretend you weren't looking at your emails if you're fighting back vomit.

I was in a total panic for days. When I met with my manager the following week, I came in with a list of excuses for why I couldn't get the engineer's work done. With a puzzled look on her face, she said "You're not an engineer, why would you ever think you would have to do this stuff?"

When we run into things we have a visceral reaction against doing, whether it's event planning, coding or simply taking the garbage out, asking ourselves what's getting in our way can shed light on what's really going on inside us. Not wanting to do something is often a signal we don't have the skills to feel confident doing it, making it feel tedious and time consuming. It also might be a sign we're not the right person for the job—remember our chapter on reframing accountability?

With event planning, I could solicit a few volunteers who enjoy this living hell to take on the areas that made me most anxious. With the engineer, I jumped into fixer mode without stopping to think if I was the right person to handle the job. Stopping to determine what was getting in the way and causing the stress and then making small adjustments would have gone miles to make these difficult situations more doable.

The next time you get stuck, consider: How can I surface what I learned about myself, unleash new options and uncover what is getting in the way of feeling confident or capable? With your reframing tools in your back pocket and these myths busted, it's time to get the hell out there and go after what you want. Tell that inner critic to shut the fuck up and get out of your way, start advocating for yourself and go for what really matters to you.

IT WILL BE WORTH IT.

AFTERWORD

IT'S AN ODD FEELING to write an ending for a book about a topic that is very much in progress. Some days I have the strength to get unstuck and immediately pick up my frames of confidence, self-assuredness and presence. And then, many times, given that I am a human being with flaws and all, I revert. I stay stuck. I need a little reminder. You may find this is true of yourself as well. All I ask is for you to give it a try. Take from here what has been useful and meet yourself with a little compassion, knowing that perfect isn't the goal. Life is as exhausting as it is exhilarating, and just like my random eviction text that started this story, things can change in an instant. So can your perspective.

This book started with an idea. I opened my laptop, and the words began to flow. It wasn't easy to find time to write with a baby, a full-time job and a move to a new city, but I just kept typing. I didn't have a clue what would become of it, if I would even get more than a few chapters on paper, if people would find it interesting, if it would ever turn into something real. But it did. That says less about me than it does the power of focus and the benefit of just going for it. It also proves that seeing your big idea come to fruition is completely achievable for you, too.

If you wanted me to end this saying I'm healed now and never struggle with the challenges of feedback, comparison, confidence, conflict...then you're giving me more credit than I deserve. Each of the stories I've shared represents a moment in time, and with new stressors and in new situations, all of this shit gets complicated all over again. Thanks, life.

Reframing isn't about convincing ourselves that none of this stuff is going to happen ever again. Double standards, biases and inequities will be ever-present even as we continue to fight against them. But reframing allows you to approach these challenges from a new starting point, saying, "Yes, this is what's present, and here's how I'm going to look at the situation, or here's what I'm going to do despite it." It makes all of this hard stuff feel doable, (to use a ridiculous example) like a 30-minute spin class as opposed to a 90-minute one where we have to bring a change of clothes and snacks just to get through the session. It gives us a tool that allows us to question a situation *instead* of questioning our own worth and value within that situation. The more we practice that, the more we shift our perspective instead of changing ourselves, the more resilient we become.

Life is exciting when there's a bit of spice to it; we just don't need to be auditioning for an episode of *Hot Ones*, choking on a ghost pepper every time we receive a passive aggressive email from a douchey colleague. Instead of letting "as per my last email" ruin your day and start a loop of feeling like you're never enough, remember that's *that* person's journey, not yours. Use it as ammunition for your TikToks.

As you finish this book and start to think of the list of goals you have for yourself (hell yes!) and things you want to try out at work (go go go!), toss aside the frame of fear that you can't do it all or don't have enough time and pick up the frame of gratitude that stems from the fact that you now know how to move forward when you get stuck. You might have to do one of my reframing exercises 15 times a day at first, but slowly it will become 10 times, then eight times, then five, and you'll find you've built up the muscle to look at situations you are faced with through a perspective that best serves you.

To get unstuck, we must continually ask ourselves, *What else is possible?* This doesn't just apply to our own shit. Reframing our perspectives fosters empathy for ourselves as well as others (even the passive aggressive email sender...hey, maybe they had a really tough morning). Since we are constantly changing and evolving, the way we view challenges, wins, accomplishments and pitfalls will also shift. Everyone else is *also* going through this constant state of change. No one is perfect and there's always more going on with someone behind the scenes than we're privy to. Our reframe away from judgment opens the door to curiosity, to wondering *what* is going on in someone's life as opposed to *why* they are a certain way. Survey Troll, I forgive you.

Tackling these challenges is so much harder than it needs to be if we go at it alone, if we believe in the myth that no one else is going through these things, that there is something wrong with us and us alone. If anything I shared in this book resonated with you, then you see you are certainly not alone. Talk to more women, learn about their experiences, hear your experiences in their stories, your pain in their struggles. The more we remember we are all connected, the less we compete, the less we criticize and the faster we all rise.

We began this book with the story of a text message that changed everything. What started as a situation that could have completely knocked me on my ass ended up being better than I could have asked for. Had I not gotten that text, would I have set out on the course to making the move and taking the reins on my career? Maybe not. In that situation, and across all 12 challenges that we explored, had I gotten stuck thinking *I can't handle this, it's too much, I'm not strong enough* and not taken action, would I have had the strength to reframe? Nope. And had I convinced myself I needed to go at it alone, even when I had the potential support of my manager, colleagues and all of the tools we've discussed throughout the book, would I have landed in the better place I ended up and finally started to quiet the inner critic? Nope again.

The lesson of this book isn't that there's some magical force outside yourself that can make all of your problems disappear, but that you actually have that magical force *within you* to get unstuck via the power of reframing: Spidey sense 2.0. You now know what to look out for, what to listen to and how to notice the limiting perspectives that surface when you're staring down a challenge. Remember that there is always a path forward, and the new perspective we approach a challenge with that contains more awareness of ourselves, our realities, our goals, our values and our interests is always better than the perspective we had available on autopilot.

Life is complex, full of moments of joy, excitement, pain and disappointment. Many of these feelings are all happening at the same time. So much of the journey is in how we perceive it, in the frame through which we choose to look at the world. I know you can accomplish whatever goals you set for yourself. But you don't have to prove it to me. And you certainly don't need to prove it to your science teacher from ninth grade who judged you for mixing up Rhodium and Rhenium on the periodic table (as if anyone knows the fucking difference), your colleague who loves to mansplain your points even though they were clear the first time you said them (thanks, Tom) or your shitty boss who has you do all of the work for none of the credit (not bitter).

It's time to prove it to yourself.

You are not stuck; you are grounded. You are not stuck; you are rooted. You are not stuck; you are growing and evolving with a firm understanding of who you are and who you want to be.

Go be it.

NOTES

FOREWORD
Martin, Courtney E. *Perfect Girls, Starving Daughters*. New York: Berkley Books, 2008.

CHAPTER 1 HOW IT BEGAN
Brown, Brené. *Daring Greatly: How the Courage to Be Vulnerable Transforms the Way We Live, Love, Parent, and Lead*. New York: Avery, an Imprint of Penguin Random House, 2015.
Doyle, Glennon. *Untamed*. New York: The Dial Press, 2020.

CHAPTER 2 REFRAMING FEEDBACK
Hastings, Reed, and Erin Meyer. *No Rules Rules: Netflix and the Culture of Reinvention*. London: VH Allen, 2020.
Helgesen, Sally, and Marshall Goldsmith. *How Women Rise: Break the 12 Habits Holding You Back*. London: Random House Business Books, 2019.
Mohr, Tara. *Playing Big: Find Your Voice, Your Mission, Your Message*. New York: Avery, an Imprint of Penguin Random House, 2015.
Scott, Kim. *Radical Candor: Be a Kick-Ass Boss Without Losing Your Humanity*. New York: St. Martins Press, 2019.
Stone, Douglas, and Sheila Heen. *Thanks for the Feedback: The Science and Art of Receiving Feedback Well: (Even When It Is Off Base, Unfair, Poorly Delivered, and Frankly, You're Not in the Mood)*. London: Portfolio Penguin, 2015.

CHAPTER 3 REFRAMING YOUR IMPACT
Leanse, Ellen Petry. " *'Just' Say No.*" LinkedIn (blog), May 29, 2015. http://www.linkedin.com/pulse/just-say-ellen-petry-leanse.
Mohr, Tara. *Playing Big: Find Your Voice, Your Mission, Your Message*. New York: Avery, an Imprint of Penguin Random House, 2015.

CHAPTER 4 REFRAMING YOUR GOALS
Brown, Brené. *The Gifts of Imperfection*. New York: Random House, 2020.
Burnett, William, and David J. Evans. *Designing Your Life: How to Build a Well-Lived, Joyful Life*. London: Vintage Books, 2018.
Clear, James. *Atomic Habits*. New York: Avery, 2018.
Dobrowolski, Patti. *"Draw Your Future."* Lecture at TEDxSeattle, Seattle, January 10, 2012. http://tedxseattle.com/talks/draw-your-future/.
Dweck, Carol. *"The Study of Goals in Psychology."* Psychological Science 3, no. 3 (May 1992): 165-67. citeseerx.ist.psu.edu/viewdoc/download?doi=10.1.1.946.9854&rep=rep1&type=pdf.
Grant, Adam. *Think Again*. New York: Viking, 2021.
Grant, Adam. *"When Strength Becomes Weakness."* WorkLife with Adam Grant, April 23, 2019. Podcast, 36. http://podcasts.apple.com/us/podcast/when-strength-becomes-weakness/id1346314086?i=1000436121595.

CHAPTER 5 REFRAMING CONFLICT
Brown, Brené. *Rising Strong: How the Ability to Reset Transforms the Way We Live, Love, Parent, and Lead*. New York: Random House, 2017.
Patterson, Kerry, Joseph Grenny, Ron McMillan, and Al Switzler. *Crucial Conversations*. New York: McGraw Hill, 2012.

CHAPTER 6 REFRAMING CONFIDENCE
Harris, Russ. *The Confidence Gap: From Fear to Freedom*. London: Robinson, 2011.
Kay, Katty, and Claire Shipman. *The Confidence Code: The Science and Art of Self-Assurance—What Women Should Know*. New York: HarperBusiness, an Imprint of HarperCollins Publishers, 2018.
Menendez, Alicia. *The Likeability Trap*. New York: HarperCollins Publishers, 2019.
Mohr, Tara. *Playing Big: Find Your Voice, Your Mission, Your Message*. New York: Avery, an Imprint of Penguin Random House, 2015.
Petri, Alexandra. *"Famous quotes, the way a woman would have to say them during a meeting."* *The Washington Post*, October 13, 2015. http://www.washingtonpost.com/blogs/compost/wp/2015/10/13/jennifer-lawrence-has-a-point-famous-quotes-the-way-a-woman-

would-have-to-say-them-during-a-meeting/.

Simmons, Rachel. *Enough as She Is: How to Help Girls Move Beyond Impossible Standards of Success to Live Healthy, Happy, and Fulfilling Lives*. New York: Harper, 2019.

CHAPTER 7 REFRAMING YOUR VALUE

Hauser, Fran. *The Myth of the Nice Girl: Harnessing the Untapped Strength of Kindness to Succeed on Your Own Terms*. Boston: Houghton Mifflin Harcourt Publishing Company, 2018.

Manson, Mark. *The Subtle Art of Not Giving a F*ck: A Counterintuitive Approach to Living a Good Life*. New York: HarperLuxe, 2019.

Menendez, Alicia. *The Likeability Trap*. New York: HarperCollins Publishers, 2019.

CHAPTER 8 REFRAMING NEGOTIATING

Carter, Alexandra. *Ask for More: 10 Questions to Ask to Get What You Want*. London: Simon and Schuster, 2020.

Ferriss, Tim. "How Creatives Should Negotiate." The Tim Ferriss Show, June 15, 2016. Podcast, 1:40:41. http://tim.blog/2016/06/15/how-creatives-should-negotiate/.

Fisher, Roger, and William Ury. *Getting to Yes: Negotiating Agreement without Giving in*. New York: Penguin, 2011.

HP 2013 Living Progress Report. Report. h20195.www2.hp.com/v2/getpdf.aspx/c05348527.pdf.

CHAPTER 9 REFRAMING THE EGO

Adams, Marilee. *Change Your Questions, Change Your Life: 12 Powerful Tools for Life and Work*. San Francisco: Berrett-Koehler Publishers, Inc., 2016.

Boshoff, Alison. "March of the Bigfoot celebs: Why DO so many famous women have such monster feet?" Daily Mail, April 14, 2015. http://www.dailymail.co.uk/femail/article-3039072/March-Bigfoot-celebs-famous-women-monster-feet.html.

Dalio, Ray. Principles. New York: Simon and Schuster, 2017.

Dhawan, Erica. *Digital Body Language: How to Build Trust & Connection, No Matter the Distance*. London: HarperCollins Publishers, 2021.

Lexico. http://www.lexico.com/en/definition/ego.

Robbins, Mike. *Nothing Changes Until You Do: A Guide to Self-Compassion and Getting Out of Your Own Way*. Carlsbad, CA: Hay House, 2014.

CHAPTER 10 REFRAMING FAILURE

Courey, Sarah, Jess Huang, Ankur Kumar, Sara Prince, Alexis Krivkovich, and Lareina Yee. *Women in the Workplace*. Report. September 30, 2020. http://www.mckinsey.com/featured-insights/diversity-and-inclusion/women-in-the-workplace.

Dweck, Carol S. *Mindset: The New Psychology of Success*. New York: Ballantine Books, 2008.

Hastings, Reed, and Erin Meyer. *No Rules Rules: Netflix and the Culture of Reinvention*. London: VH Allen, 2020.

Helgesen, Sally, and Marshall Goldsmith. *How Women Rise: Break the 12 Habits Holding You Back*. London: Random House Business Books, 2019.

CHAPTER 11 REFRAMING ACCOUNTABILITY

Brown, Brené. *The Gifts of Imperfection*. New York: Random House, 2020.

Lencioni, Patrick. *The Five Dysfunctions of a Team*. New York: Random House, 2002.

Nagoski, Emily, and Amelia Nagoski. *Burnout: The Secret to Unlocking the Stress Cycle*. New York: Ballantine Books, 2020.

Obama, Michelle. *Becoming*. New York: Crown, an Imprint of the Crown Publishing Group, 2018.

CHAPTER 12 REFRAMING DECISION-MAKING

Harris, Russ. *The Confidence Gap: From Fear to Freedom*. London: Robinson, 2011.

Heath, Chip, and Dan Heath. *Decisive: How to Make Better Choices in Life and Work*. London: Random House Business, 2014.

CHAPTER 13 REFRAMING COMPARISON

Brown, Brené. *The Gifts of Imperfection*. New York: Random House, 2020.

Harris, Russ. *The Confidence Gap: From Fear to Freedom*. London: Robinson, 2011.

Simmons, Rachel. *Enough as She Is: How to Help Girls Move Beyond Impossible Standards of Success to Live Healthy, Happy, and Fulfilling Lives*. New York: Harper, 2019.

INDEX

ACKNOWLEDGEMENTS

THANK YOU TO everyone who helped shape my path and bring to life the vision that was *Unstuck*.

My family: my parents, Helen and Larry, who have given me unconditional support in anything I wanted to go after; my sister, Zoe, who has been a lifelong mentor and friend no matter what life throws at us; Bonnie, Cindy, Chris, Jim, David and Bill, my aunts and uncles who have always seen the creative spark in me and encouraged me to go for it even when my ideas were way out there; my cousins Peter, Alison, Troy and Yanni and brothers-in-law Sal and Ted for being my second set of siblings (and some of the few people before this book who knew how my inner thoughts actually sounded); Mimi, whose energy, spark and knowledge of pop culture at 92 puts all of us to shame and, of course, my husband, Wes, and daughter, Maya, who bring meaning and joy into every moment of my life.

My managers and colleagues: Ben, who cultivated my passion for creating fun and collaborative team cultures; Bojana and Mathew, who, beyond being mentors, celebrated my Spidey sense and propensity to ask unpopular questions; Simmons, who motivates women to question the expectations thrown at us and be our full selves; Jon, Elizabeth and JT, who "yes and-ed" all of my big, bold ideas; and Rachel, the person with unshakable confidence in me who saw how to harness my passion into transformational work and encouraged me to carve my own path (and, spoiler: the one who helped me talk about my book without laughing).

My fantastic support system of fellow women in tech, some brave enough to be early readers of this book: Luci, Cathy, Kellyn, Cassandra, Lulu, Sophie, Kristina, Elisa, Shelby, Angela, Terry, Nidhi, Trashawn, Megan, Sharifa, Nikki, Staci, Tracie, Nicole, Carla, Sarah, Lauren, Sharon. You are an inspiration and fuel my passion for making sure women like you are seen and celebrated.

Patrick, my first editor, who gave me confidence this book could be something. Katherine and Paul, my coach and teacher who encouraged me to trust my instincts and be brave and true to myself. Mary, one of my closest friends and longest proponents of my writing.

Thank you to my team at Media Lab Books: Phil, who took a chance on me and acquired this book and whose guidance and support has made what could have been a stressful process fun and exciting. Jeff, who got me to break out of my shell and go full Lia. Jules, who wove the right amount of authority into my tone. Susan, whose design prowess brought this to life. And to Courtney: thank you for working around the clock to get this book done, entering into my brain and knowing exactly what I meant to say when something was confusing, artfully making the complicated sound simple and being the only person on Earth able to make feedback a gift. I am so lucky to have worked with you.

 **LIA GARVIN** is an operations leader, speaker and coach on a mission to humanize the workplace, one conversation at a time. Through her writing, leadership coaching and savvy program management skills, she brings an authentic and irreverent sense of humor to teams to help them examine the challenges holding them back and focus on what matters. She has built robust diversity and inclusion programs, launched the world's first holographic computer and driven programs and initiatives around team inclusion and organizational effectiveness across her work in tech; and coaches people on how to drive impactful work and thrive while working in the corporate world. She was recognized by the National Diversity Council as a 2021 DEI Champion.

Lia is the author of *UNSTUCK: Reframe Your Thinking to Free Yourself From the Patterns and People That Hold You Back*, leaning into nearly 10 years of experience working at some of the largest and most influential companies in tech including Microsoft, Apple and Google to explore the power of reframing to overcome common challenges found in the modern workplace. She has a Bachelor of Arts from UCLA in Sociology, a Master of Arts from the New College of California in Media Studies and is a Co-Active- and ICF-certified professional coach. She also holds a certification in Hatha yoga, because why not?

When she is not stirring things up at work, Lia enjoys writing articles about building effective teams, reading organizational culture books while walking on her treadmill (multitasking: it's a lifestyle) and spending time with her family.

Media Lab Books
For inquiries, call 646-838-6637

Copyright 2022 Topix Media Lab

Published by Topix Media Lab
14 Wall Street, Suite 4B
New York, NY 10005

Printed in China

ISBN-13: 978-1-948174-88-6
ISBN-10: 1-948174-88-X

CEO Tony Romando

Vice President & Publisher Phil Sexton
Senior Vice President of Sales & New Markets Tom Mifsud
Vice President of Retail Sales & Logistics Linda Greenblatt
Chief Financial Officer Vandana Patel
Manufacturing Director Nancy Puskuldjian
Financial Analyst Matthew Quinn
Digital Marketing & Strategy Manager Elyse Gregov

Chief Content Officer Jeff Ashworth
Director of Editorial Operations Courtney Kerrigan
Creative Director Susan Dazzo
Photo Director Dave Weiss
Executive Editor Tim Baker

Content Editor Juliana Sharaf
Senior Editor Trevor Courneen
Assistant Managing Editor Tara Sherman
Designers Glen Karpowich, Mikio Sakai
Copy Editor & Fact Checker Madeline Raynor
Junior Designer Alyssa Bredin Quirós

Cover photo: Shutterstock
Photo illustration: Eric Heintz

Indexing by Meridith Murray

1C-L21-1